Phonics Fundamentals

Phonics Fundamentals

Everything you need to know to teach phonics

Amy-Louise Peach

1 Oliver's Yard
55 City Road
London EC1Y 1SP

2455 Teller Road
Thousand Oaks
California 91320

10th Floor, Emaar Capital Tower 2
MG Road, Sikanderpur, Sector 26
Gurugram, Haryana – 122002
India

8 Marina View Suite 43-053
Asia Square Tower 1
Singapore 018960

© 2026 Amy-Louise Peach

Apart from any fair dealing for the purposes of research or private study, or criticism or review, as permitted under the Copyright, Designs and Patents Act 1988, this publication may be reproduced, stored or transmitted in any form, or by any means, only with the prior permission in writing of the publishers, or in the case of reprographic reproduction, in accordance with the terms of licences issued by the Copyright Licensing Agency. Enquiries concerning reproduction outside those terms should be sent to the publishers.

Editor: Amy Thornton
Senior project editor: Chris Marke
Cover design: Wendy Scott
Typeset by: C&M Digitals (P) Ltd, Chennai, India

Library of Congress Control Number: 2025939862

British Library Cataloguing in Publication data

A catalogue record for this book is available from the British Library

ISBN 978-1-0362-1445-6
ISBN 978-1-0362-1444-9 (pbk)

Contents

About the author vii

Introduction: what is phonics? 1

Part 1

1 Phase One 15
2 Phase Two 29
3 Phase Three and Phase Four 43
4 Phase Five and Phase Six 59

Part 2

5 Phonics screening check 81
6 Phonics in provision 95
7 Supporting phonics learning for children with special educational needs and disabilities 103
8 Working with parents and carers 111
9 Further support 117

Jargon buster glossary 121
References 133
Index 137

About the author

Amy-Louise Peach is a qualified teacher, education consultant and content creator. She is passionate about phonics and early reading. Amy-Louise started a YouTube channel, Little Learners Videos, to support families and provide easy-to-understand videos to make the world of phonics less confusing. Over time, the channel grew to cover more areas of learning and reach families and professionals across the world. Amy-Louise built on this and started her business – Little Learners Education™ – through which she works as an education consultant, helping families, teachers, childminders and other professionals to support children with their phonics journeys.

Introduction

What is phonics?

Phonics is at the core of so much we do as early educators, whether you're in Early Years or primary school. For teachers – experienced or early career teacher (ECT) – Early Years practitioners, teaching assistants, learning support assistants and an ongoing list of educators, understanding the fundamentals of systematic synthetic phonics is vital to ensure we are giving the children in our care the very best education and opportunities possible. From learning to listen to and explore sounds, to reading words and writing stories, phonics forms a crucial part of a child's education.

So why, then, do so many of us as educators feel underprepared when it comes to this topic? If you're anything like me, you entered the classroom for the first time with a very limited knowledge of phonics. Maybe you were able to observe phonics teaching during your training, or even teach some phonics lessons. Perhaps you had hardly seen any phonics teaching before. For many of us, clinging onto our setting's chosen phonics scheme for dear life is the only way we make it through that first year. It can feel as though you are learning along with the children (although being just enough ahead of them to make it look like you know what you're doing), hoping week-to-week that you will pick it all up eventually. Then you do. You understand the scheme, the order in which the letters and sounds are taught, and how children progress through the scheme as you move forward. But what happens when you move to a new scheme? What happens when a child isn't progressing in the way you would expect and you have to devise some phonics intervention for them? Without knowing those fundamentals, you have no foundation to fall back on. You're in a very specific box, when really you deserve to have the confidence to break free of those limits and become an artist with phonics, using a variety of mediums to create something unique for that child, in order to help them flourish and paint with all the colours of the alphabet.

When I trained to become a teacher, my PGCE was in Primary Education – not Early Years. It's strange to think of now, as I can't imagine doing anything other than my current career, working as an Early Years specialist, consultant and content creator. My journey began as a Reception class teacher, but that wasn't the plan. I had been offered a position in Key Stage 1, but this had to be changed last minute due to staff timetables. I was terrified, having to learn an entirely new framework over the summer and diving into the world of phonics. Turns out, I loved it. Early Years quickly became my passion and I fell in love with teaching phonics.

Most of the parents and carers of my students had no idea what phonics was, let alone how to support their children with it at home. They mispronounced sounds, got confused when their four-year-olds started coming out with words like 'digraph' and didn't understand why learning to read seemed so different now, compared to their own experience of school. And who can blame them? Education has changed so much over the years and practice is constantly evolving. If we didn't tell parents and carers what was going on, how were they to know? I began making YouTube videos to support parents and carers with phonics, going back to the basics (the fundamentals, if you will), and soon realised that educators also watched my videos. I've had the pleasure of speaking with so many teachers, home educators, teaching assistants, nursery practitioners and other educators, and one thread that weaves through almost all of those conversations is needing support with phonics. I made more videos to keep up with this need, and my YouTube channel grew to over 300,000 subscribers. I began consulting, working with companies, tutoring and continuing to support families and educators all over the world. I was once sent a video from a school in Nigeria, which showed a whole class of children using my videos to learn phonics, 3,000 miles away. This career has truly been the most rewarding experience and I am so grateful that I get to do it every day.

Becoming an Early Years specialist and phonics fanatic didn't come easy, though. My PGCE barely covered phonics, even though it was preparing us to teach children aged five to 11. Phonics is so important throughout primary school and even beyond, yet we were not given the gift of learning about this complex subject. My PGCE experience was ten years ago now, so I'd like to think things are better than they were. Don't get me wrong – my PGCE and the university I studied at were incredible. We learnt so much, had supportive and knowledgeable lecturers and received a very high (if not completely daunting, stressful and at times all-encompassing) level of teacher training. And yet, the only mention of phonics I can recall is during one English seminar, when the lecturer mentioned some schemes and that phonics was used to teach children to read. When I went into schools to do my teaching practice, I was placed in Year 4 and then Year 2. I didn't have the chance to see much phonics teaching at this stage, as most of the children were working at Phase Five and beyond. Having spoken to many other educators over the years, it seems that this has been the case for a lot of us.

It's no wonder, then, that so many teachers feel overwhelmed by teaching phonics. The last newly qualified teacher (NQT) survey was conducted by the Department for Education (DfE) in 2017. It showed that only 63 per cent of new teachers felt prepared to teach students to read and only 39 per cent felt confident in teaching children with English as an additional language (Ginnis et al., 2018), for which phonics plays a big role. In 2019, YouGov (conducting research on behalf of Ofsted) found that only 13 per cent of teachers in primary schools felt that all teaching staff had the necessary experience in teaching phonics for all children to make progress. Thirteen per cent! That is an incredibly low number that reflects just how much of a systemic problem this is, and the injustice our training programmes are doing – not only to our early educators, but also to the children they will come to teach. Due to the replacement of the NQT programme with the ECT programme in 2021, we have been left waiting for more up-to-date data in this area. However, the early data about the effectiveness of the switch to the ECT programme doesn't provide much evidence that things have changed.

So if you are reading this book because you lack confidence in phonics, you are not alone! This book is your go-to guide for all things phonics, to understand the fundamentals that systematic synthetic phonics and the various schemes out there are built upon. Written by an educator for educators, think of this book as the friend who has the answers to all of your phonics questions. While I would recommend reading it in order from beginning to end, please feel free to jump around chapters to find that piece of information you need *right now*. Just don't forget to come back and build up that knowledge right from the foundation.

The importance of phonics should not be underestimated. Of the seven areas of learning in the Early Years Foundation Stage (EYFS), phonics can first be found in the prime area 'Communication and language' and then in the specific area 'Literacy' (DfE, 2024b). Without skills in the three prime areas of learning, children are unable to access learning in the specific areas. If a child cannot listen, attend and understand, they will find it extremely difficult to go through the process of learning letter sounds, sounding out words and reading sentences. Listening, attention and understanding skills transcend just one area of learning though; they are necessary in all areas of learning in one way or another. When it comes to early learning goals (ELGs, a set of 17 statements children are assessed against at the end of the Reception year), 'Word reading' within Literacy is phonics' most obvious home, but certainly not its only one. When children transition to the national curriculum, phonics continues to be a focus to support children to become fluent readers with a wide vocabulary. As in the EYFS, these skills are not limited to one subject, as the national curriculum explains: 'fluency in the English language is an essential foundation for success in all subjects' (DfE, 2013).

Systematic synthetic phonics

'Systematic synthetic phonics' is the full name for the method we use to teach children to read. If it sounds confusing, then don't worry. We can break this down further:

- *systematic*: a structured system. The 'structure' we use in phonics teaching mostly refers to the phases of phonics (which we'll get onto later), as well as the order in which we teach sounds and how children progress through their phonics learning;
- *synthetic*: synthesising refers to combining sounds. In phonics, this translates to putting sounds together in order to read whole words. We call this 'blending', which we'll discuss later in this chapter;
- *phonics*: matching the sound (phoneme) to the written letter (grapheme). For example, the letter 'a' makes the /a/ sound, such as in 'cat'.

Now that we understand the meaning behind the name, systematic synthetic phonics (SSP) can be defined like so: the method we use to teach children to read, by matching sounds to their corresponding written letters, in a structured way, to put those sounds together and read whole words.

Why did we start using systematic synthetic phonics?

At this point you may be thinking back to your own education. *Did I learn to read using phonics? How did I even learn to read in the first place?* I have found that many adults remember learning to read by *rote learning*, which involves memorising words by sight through repetition. It wasn't until 1998 that the government included phonics in its National Literacy Strategy. However, this was simply guidance and was not statutory, so many schools continued to use rote learning, or used a combination of both approaches. Schemes like Lyn Wendon's 'Letterland' grew in popularity from 1975, with schools gravitating to schemes such as this one for children with special educational needs. Over time, educators noticed that this way of teaching could benefit all students. In 2006, it became a legal requirement for schools to use the systematic synthetic phonics approach to teach children to read (*Guardian*, 2006). Not everyone was on board, as with many changes in education (or change in general), but in 2007 the DfE published guidance for schools to follow called *Letters and Sounds*, outlining a clear system of progression throughout a child's phonics learning journey. Schools either adapted this to create their own phonics programmes or bought into a phonics scheme.

Why do we teach phonics?

Even though phonics wasn't always the go-to for teaching reading, children still managed to learn how to read. We don't have generations of adults without any reading skills. So why did we change things? Why do we teach phonics in the way that we do now?

If we learn the letter names of the alphabet, we can't really use that knowledge to decode words. Rote learning can work for many children, memorising a wide variety of words, increasing in complexity as the child progresses through their reading journey. However, this way of learning can make it difficult to read unfamiliar words. With rote learning, a child doesn't necessarily learn why a word sounds the way it does, or why it is spelt the way it is. If a child comes across a new word without the ability to sound it out to decode it, they are limited in their ability to read new words, make those connections and become a more independent reader.

With systematic synthetic phonics, we start right from the beginning. Children are given the tools they need to decode words; tools they can use forever, no matter when they come across a new word. For example, knowing how to read the word 'pats' through rote learning gives the child access to that one word. However, learning the individual sounds for each letter (/p/, /a/, /t/ and /s/) allows the child to read more words, such as 'sat', 'pat', 'tap', 'taps' and so on. Using a systematic approach with *phases* gives children a solid foundation on which to build future phonics learning. The reason I'm so passionate about phonics is because of the power it holds and the fact that we as educators can give this power to children and allow them to become strong, independent readers who can not only decode words in an increasingly accurate and fluent way, but who can also discover a love for reading and unlock an entire world of information, interesting facts, wonderful stories, delicious recipes and so much more.

Phonics and SEND

For children with certain special educational needs and disabilities (SEND), phonics can be a more accessible way to learn how to read. With a gradual and progressive approach, phonics as a system can be tailored to a child's needs, with some children spending much more time on one phase, or even one set of letter sounds. For minimally verbal and non-verbal children, there are still many ways they can access phonics and engage in the phases, from matching games to following with their finger as an adult reads, assigning actions to sounds, interacting with props, typing, implementing technology such as speech devices, using symbols and much more. Similarly, for children who have English as an additional language (EAL), phonics supports them in learning and understanding the way the English language works and how its words are constructed.

If a school chooses to use a scheme for phonics, there are a variety to suit different learning styles. For example, *Jolly Phonics* (Jolly Learning, 1987) is a popular scheme which uses actions, songs, letters and sounds to support children with a range of learning styles to learn sounds. Not only can this be beneficial for children with particular SEND, it can work for a whole class of learners.

Letters and Sounds

Phonics as a system is usually referred to as having six phases. These phases guide us through the different stages of phonics, allowing children to progress in a way that builds on prior knowledge. Phonics phases originated in the *Letters and Sounds* guidance (DfE, 2007). This was not designed to be a full scheme, but rather something for schools and companies to build from when creating their own. Therefore, most phonics schemes follow this six-phase model. Even though phonics schemes can differ in their approach, the thread running through most of them comes from the original *Letters and Sounds* guidance.

Phonics phases

We will look closely at each phase in the following chapters, but let's get a general sense of what they are first.

- *Phase One* is our starting point. This comes before any letters are learnt, instead focusing on sound discrimination by building children's listening skills, involving environmental sounds, spoken sounds, body percussion and instrumental sounds.
- *Phase Two* is what we often think of when we say 'phonics'. This usually starts at the beginning of the Reception year, with children learning several sounds per week. The sounds are not taught in alphabetical order, instead starting with /s/ /a/ /t/ /p/ /i/ and /n/, also known among educators as 'satpin' or 'satnip'. The reason we begin with these sounds, rather than /a/ /b/ /c/ and so on, is so that children can start to read more words more quickly. We'll go into that more in Chapter 2. Children will now start to learn *tricky words*, also known as *common-exception words* or *sight words*. These are words that cannot be decoded using phonics, so must be learnt by sight. In this case, rote learning sneaks in.
- *Phase Three* follows on from Phase Two, introducing more new sounds and the concept of *digraphs*, which are two letters making one sound, such as the /ch/ in 'chip'. We also come across *trigraphs* in this phase, such as the /igh/ in 'light'. Children cover more tricky words at this stage.
- When we reach *Phase Four*, no new sounds are introduced. Instead, children focus on practising the letter sounds they have already learnt, and using this knowledge to decode words with more than one syllable. 'Alien words' are often introduced at this stage, which are nonsense words (such as 'lig' or 'taff') used to assess if a child can sound out a word they have never come across before. Again, children learn new tricky words in this phase.
- *Phase Five* focuses on alternative pronunciations and spellings to those that children have already learnt. For example, they will know at this stage the /ai/ sound in 'paint', but will now learn that we can also make the same sound with 'a' and 'y', such as in 'play'. Similarly, children will learn that some graphemes make more than one sound, such as /ow/ in 'cow' and /ow/ in 'slow'. More tricky words are also introduced.
- *Phase Six* is our final phonics phase and focuses on developing fluency and accuracy when reading. Children will be able to read some familiar words without decoding them and be more confident decoding new words.

Segmenting and blending

Decoding words or *sounding out* involves two skills: *segmenting* and *blending*. In order to read a word, the child must first break it up (segment) into its smallest units of sound, called *phonemes*. For example, the word 'pan' would be segmented into the phonemes /p/ /a/ /n/ and the word 'ship' would be segmented into /sh/ /i/ /p/. Many educators choose to implement 'robot arms' at this stage. For each letter sound spoken, children move one arm up and one arm down, with their elbows at their sides, like a robot. This movement can help children who are struggling with segmenting to really focus on each individual sound. As we know, not all children learn in the same way, so this combination of seeing the letter, saying the sound, hearing the sound and using movement can support a range of different learners. Once children are confident in segmenting, they can move onto the next skill of blending. Not only do children need to use their knowledge of letters and their corresponding sounds, they also need to use their listening skills to hear each sound and blend them together in order to read the whole word. Blending is a skill that often takes a little longer to develop than segmenting. It can help to say the sounds out loud, then repeat them but speed up a little each time. The quicker you say the sounds, the closer they come together and eventually you will simply say the word.

Activity to understand how blending works

Let's take the word 'chomp'. First, segment the word into its phonemes and say them aloud:

/ch/ /o/ /m/ /p/

Now, say the sounds again, but a little faster. Can you hear the difference? What if you say them even more quickly? Does it become harder to distinguish between the different sounds as they blend together?

The schwa

With any new skill, there are going to be mistakes. It's a natural part of learning. However, there is one mistake we as educators must be sure not to make, as it can have a devastating effect on children's ability to sound out words. It is a mistake I see all too often, and one that makes me shudder whenever I hear it! This mistake is the *schwa*.

Technically, a schwa is a reduced mid-central vowel, most commonly referring to /ə/ in the international phonetic alphabet. Put more simply though, the schwa is the utterance 'uh'. The reason we need to know about this little sound is because it can cause havoc if it's used incorrectly when teaching phonics, adding an extra sound to letters when it isn't needed. Let's take a look at the most likely offenders:

f   l   m   n   r   s   t   v

These certainly aren't all the letters that can be affected, but the most common I've seen in my practice. How do you pronounce each of these letters? Some may pronounce them like this:

'fuh'   'luh'   'muh'   'nuh'   'ruh'   'suh'   'tuh'   'vuh'

These are the incorrect pronunciations for these letters. 'But Amy!' I hear you cry, 'That's how I learnt them at school!' and yes, that may be true. I learnt to pronounce these sounds with schwas when I was at school, too. However, as phonics teaching has evolved, so has our knowledge of how to teach it. Let's look at the word 'mat'. If sounded out with schwas, we get this:

/muh/ /a/ /tuh/

When blended together, we get 'muhatuh' – a word with two extra phonemes, that sounds much more like 'matter' than 'mat'. If we sound the word out again but with the correct pronunciations, we get:

/m/ /a/ /t/

This can be easily blended to make the word 'mat', with just three phonemes. Hopefully you can see how troublesome schwas can be and how they can really hinder a child's ability to blend and read accurately. Fear not, though: throughout this book we will be identifying the correct pronunciations for each letter sound.

Validation

When it comes to choosing the method schools or settings want to use to teach phonics, there is no statutory requirement for them to use a particular scheme. While the DfE does provide a list of validated schemes, which it deems as meeting the criteria for an effective systematic synthetic phonics programme, schools are free to create their own approach, or use a programme not on the validation list. Whatever approach a school uses, it must ensure that the programme is 'rigorous, systematic and used with fidelity' (DfE, 2024a). Naturally, most schools and settings will choose to use a scheme validated by the DfE, to ensure their phonics provision will meet all of the DfE's requirements. In order to be validated, these schemes must have been self-assessed by their publisher, as well as by a panel. The DfE states that a complete systematic synthetic phonics programme includes everything needed to teach children in Reception and Key Stage 1, enough support to encourage fluency in reading, structure that allows progression in order to meet or exceed the expectations of the Year 1 phonics screening check and all word-reading expectations set out by the national curriculum by the end of Key Stage 1.

The DfE has also selected English hubs around the country. This is a group of (at the time of writing) 34 schools that the DfE recognised for their expertise in phonics. These hubs can provide support to their local schools by developing action plans to implement phonics effectively in their setting.

Letters and Sounds revised

Before we move on, it's probably a good idea to discuss 'Little Wandle Letters and Sounds Revised' (available at www.littlewandlelettersandsounds.org.uk/). This is a scheme that was validated in 2021. The scheme was created by Little Sutton Primary School and Chesterton Primary School (an English hub), which are part of the Wandle Learning Trust. The scheme has 'revised' the *Letters and Sounds* (DfE, 2007) guidance, changing some of its components. Most notably, Phase One has been replaced by 'Foundation for phonics', and the content of Phase Two and Phase Three are different, with Phase Two covering more sounds, including many from the original Phase Three. Phase Three learning starts later and there is no Phase Six. There are two reasons to mention this: the first being the name, with *Letters and Sounds* and 'Letters and Sounds Revised' being similar and therefore easily confused; and the second being if an educator comes across this scheme, or begins working in a school or setting that uses it, they will need to know the difference when it comes to the phases. While we will be focusing on the original *Letters and Sounds* (DfE, 2007) phase system in this book, the fundamentals are the same and, having read the following chapters, you will still have the knowledge you need to teach systematic synthetic phonics.

So now we know what systematic synthetic phonics is and a bit about its history. Knowing where phonics came from and how it has evolved over time gives us a better understanding of why we teach it and how it works, as well as why certain mistakes may be made and how to rectify them. As you move through the following chapters, remember this short history lesson and apply it to what you learn next. To know where we're going, we need to know where we've been. This is true not only of phonics as an approach, but also in order to understand the progression a child will make through the phases. We need to know how phases relate to and build upon each other, how to identify gaps in learning and what to do to fill them, so we can continue to build upon a sturdy foundation of knowledge. Phonics truly is the key to opening so many doors for a child, which is why I am so pleased you are reading this book, wanting to give the gift of reading to the children in your care.

PART 1

Part 1 discusses the six-phase structure of systematic synthetic phonics (SSP). The phases begin from birth, with children learning listening and communication skills to build a solid foundation in Phase One. In Phases Two and Three, children learn how letters are pronounced and how to use segmenting and blending to read words. Moving onto Phase Four, children develop their skills further to read more complex words and a wider variety of texts. Phase Five introduces alternative spellings and pronunciations and, finally, Phase Six focuses on becoming more fluent and confident readers.

The progression through the phases does not have to be linear, as children may need to revisit skills from previous stages to address misconceptions or develop skills that were missed. Understanding the importance of each phase allows practitioners to become successful phonics teachers, able to support children in their phonics journey in the most effective way possible.

1
Phase One

This chapter will cover:

1. what Phase One is;
2. the seven aspects of Phase One;
3. activities to support Phase One learning;
4. why and how to revisit Phase One;
5. Phase One assessment.

Introduction

Phase One phonics is often forgotten by many practitioners, especially if they are teaching at Reception level and beyond. It's a shame, because Phase One is possibly the most important phase of all. There may not be any letters learnt, or words read, but without this crucial foundational phase children will be unable to move onto building their phonics skills in the future. Without Phase One, gaps in learning can begin to grow, leading to children struggling in later phases. In addition, Phase One can – and should – be used alongside later phases to support ongoing learning.

Phase One is split up into seven sections called *aspects*. Each aspect focuses on a different skill to develop children's listening, attention and understanding. Listening skills are the main focus of Phase One as without them children cannot have a foundation to build upon in further phases or the ability to access learning in other areas of development. Each aspect gives a clear area to focus on, but should not be thought of as separate; there is a lot of overlap, with skills, activities and development applying to multiple aspects at once. The aspects exist to give an idea of the order of progression in Phase One, but do not need to be followed as stand-alone. While building this foundation for phonics learning is vital, it's also important to recognise that the skill development in Phase One has value of its own, rather than simply as a stepping stone for future phases.

Each of the seven aspects is made up of three strands: tuning into sounds, listening and remembering sounds and talking about sounds.

- *tuning into sounds*: being able to tune in to sounds involves auditory discrimination; the ability to hear individual sounds, recognise them and distinguish between several different sounds happening at once;
- *listening and remembering sounds*: when developing listening skills, children work on their concentration and attention in order to hear sounds and develop recall. From birth, children are building a library of sounds they hear, then recalling these sounds and repeating them. When listening and remembering, children are developing their auditory memory and sequencing skills. Developing listening skills also involves assigning meaning to sounds, which further improves understanding and speaking skills;
- *talking about sounds*: children will need to learn a wide variety of words to build up their vocabulary, so that they can describe the sounds they hear. Autumn leaves on the ground are 'crunchy' when stepped on, drums are 'loud', mice are 'squeaky' and so on. This improves language comprehension, helps contextualise sounds and allows children to understand and talk about the sounds they hear.

Aspect 1: general sound discrimination – environmental sounds

The aim of Aspect 1 is to develop children's awareness of sounds in their environment while working on listening skills, recalling sounds and building vocabulary linked to sound. Children are exposed to hundreds of thousands of sounds, most of which happen all at once; think of a nursery setting, with the sounds of talking, playing, running, doors opening and closing, toys and resources being moved around and so on. When outside, children may hear the hustle and bustle of a busy street, with the sound of cars, crossing signals, chatting, bicycle bells and a myriad of other sounds. Before being able to discriminate between different sounds, this can all just sound like 'noise'. Being able to distinguish between these environmental sounds means children can pick out individual sounds and understand which sounds are coming together to make this noise.

Activities for Aspect 1

Activity: Listening walk

This can take place inside or outdoors (ideally both) as listening walks can happen anywhere, anytime. In this scenario we can imagine the children are in a park. Walk around and have the children observe their surroundings, so they feel comfortable. Ask them what they see, as this can help them to assign sounds to certain objects or activities later. Next, ask them to focus on what they can hear: is it loud? Quiet? Is it noisy? Encourage children to use the vocabulary they know to describe the overall sound. Next, ask the children about each sound they can hear. If they struggle to distinguish between the different sounds going on, you can model this skill by focusing on a particular sound. For example, you may ask the children to look at the trees, notice them swaying and hear the leaves rustling. Talk about what that sounds like and how it makes you feel. You may tell the children that it makes you feel calm. You may all want to sway like the trees and try to mimic the sound the rustling leaves make! Next, ask the children to close their eyes and listen again. What can they hear? Perhaps a ball bouncing, or wheels of a pushchair going by. Children may describe these sounds as 'boing boing' or 'something rattling'. Ask the children to open their eyes to identify where the sound is coming from. For children who are new to developing this skill, they may need to see the cause of each sound to distinguish it from other sounds they hear. This can also help when assigning meaning to a sound and understanding how it is made.

Activity: Sound hide and seek

A child or group of children hide and other children are the 'seekers'. To help the seekers find them, the hiders will need to make a sound. This can be a constant sound, like singing a song, or making a sound when asked (such as 'Squeak little mouse!', and the hiders

(Continued)

'squeak' in return). The seekers will need to differentiate between the different sounds they hear to tune into the sound they need to follow. Then, the seekers will follow the sound, understanding that the louder it becomes, the closer they must be to the hiders. Once everyone is found, make sure the children swap roles so that everyone has a go at being a 'sound seeker'.

Activity: Our favourite sounds

For this game, you will need pictures for the children to choose between. These pictures should show something that makes a sound; some pleasant and some not so. For example, you may have pictures of a doorbell, a barking dog, a crying baby, a bouncy ball, a child laughing and a moving car. These sounds should be relevant to the children and represent sounds they may hear in their everyday lives. This activity's aim is to encourage the children to talk about sounds. Ask the children to try making the sound associated with each picture and talk about what they do or don't like about it. A barking dog may be 'loud' or 'scary', and a child laughing may be 'happy' or 'funny'. Encourage the children to describe each sound and how it makes them feel. Then, ask the children to put the sounds in order from best to worst – or favourite to least favourite. There may be some debate here, with some children enjoying sounds others do not. This is a great teaching moment as we can explain to children that not everyone likes the same things, and that's okay. One child may like a barking dog because it reminds them of their own pet, while another may be scared of this sound because a stranger's dog once barked at them in the park. You can also introduce new vocabulary here if you feel the children don't have the words they need to describe the sound.

Aspect 2: general sound discrimination – instrumental sounds

In Aspect 2, we still focus on sound discrimination, but now introduce instruments when doing so. These can be purchased, rented or borrowed by the setting or made by the children. Many children do not have access to instruments for a variety of reasons – most notably how expensive they can be – so being able to bring instruments into the setting for children to see, listen to and explore can be a rich learning experience. As educators we must consider the socio-economic backgrounds of the children in our care when approaching Aspect 2, as children from lower-income families are 50 per cent less likely to learn how to play an instrument during childhood (Musicians' Union, 2018). However, making their own instruments is also valuable as this allows children to understand how their instrument is making its sound, based on what they used to create it.

Activities for Aspect 2

Activity: What's that instrument?

This activity should be used once children have already had the opportunity to listen to a range of different instruments and learn the names of some of them. Give the children a piece of music to listen to. Remind them of how to be good listeners: having our 'listening ears' ready and not making any noise so we can concentrate on the sounds. Ask the children what sounds they can hear within the music. This may be tricky at first, as all the instruments in the piece blend into one. Encourage children to use their growing vocabulary to describe the sounds. Next, ask them what instruments they can hear. What instrument could be making that 'banging' sound or that 'twinkly' sound? You may choose to use some pictorial clues to support the children in this task, or the actual instruments if you have access to them.

Activity: Story sounds

You may find this task is easier for the children if you use a story book that they are already familiar with. Give the children a range of instruments – these can be instruments they have made – and tell them we will play the instruments when we think the story would be making a similar sound. For example, if a story includes a thunderstorm, children may shake shakers to mimic rain and bang drums for thunder. A xylophone could be played lightly when a character is tiptoeing, and a güiro might be played as a frog croaks. It can be helpful to discuss the sounds in the book and agree what instrument should be played at certain points of the story, or when a particular word is heard.

Activity: Noise makers

This is a favourite among Early Years settings! Noise makers can be made using a range of materials and are a great way for children to understand how certain sounds can be made. A shaker can be made by filling a container such as a bottle, yogurt pots, tubes and so on with items such as rice, pasta, beads or sequins (ensure you are mindful of potential choking hazards when making the shakers). Once the container is secured with tape or a lid, children can shake it to make a sound. If children use different items to fill their shakers, they can compare the sounds they make. Another popular noise maker is the 'spin drum'. This is made by using a stick (this could be a stick found outside or something like a lolly stick or sturdy straw) and attaching it to a paper plate. Use a hole punch to make some holes around the edge of the plate. Tie a piece of string from each hole and attach a button, bead, or even pom poms (again, be mindful of choking hazards) to the end of each piece of string. As the child spins the drum back and forth, the small objects will hit either side of the plate, creating a spinning drum. Finally, a noise maker often referred to as a 'guitar' involves a box with a hole cut in the top. Stretch elastic bands over the box so that they travel across the hole. Children can 'ping' the elastic bands to make a sound, much like how guitars use strings to create music.

Aspect 3: general sound discrimination – body percussion

Now we come to noticing the different sounds our bodies can make. Using their bodies to create sound is a good way for children to start understanding rhythm, as well as becoming more aware of their own bodies. When singing songs, children can explore what happens when they sing loudly or quietly, and what they must do to make that happen (for example: 'I open my mouth wide when I'm really loud'). Singing songs and nursery rhymes is an integral part of Early Years teaching and so vocal sounds can be explored every day. You may ask the children, 'Can you sing/say this very quickly?' or 'Can you sing/say this while whispering?' Of course, our bodies can make all sort of sounds by clapping, stamping, tapping, jumping, shuffling and so on. Children should be encouraged to explore all the noises they can make with their bodies and how different actions make different sounds.

Activities for Aspect 3

Activity: Copy me

Model an action sound to children (such as a clap) and have them copy you. Tell them they must first watch and listen until you are finished, then copy you exactly (so if you only clap once, they should only clap once). Model clapping three times, two times quickly, four times softly and so on. Children may find watching, listening, remembering and copying all at once a bit tricky at first, but this helps them to tune into and recall the sounds they hear. Make this a fun experience, laughing together when we get it wrong and celebrating when we get it right. Once the children are more confident in this activity, you can add some rhythm. For example, two claps, a pause and then one more clap. You may even decide to add more than one type of sound, such as clap, clap, stomp. Once the children understand and are confident in the activity you can ask them one at a time to lead the session.

Activity: Pass it on

Have a group of children sit or stand in a circle and give them a sound to copy, such as a clap. They should 'pass on' the sound to the child next to them, until it reaches the adult again. Tell the children that the sound should stay exactly the same. Once the sound has been 'passed' around the circle, discuss what happened. Did it stay the same? Did it get louder at any point, or faster? Next, model another sound, but give the children a word to go with this sound. So, for example, 'three lazy claps', which are sloppy and slow. Next, there might be 'three excited knee taps' or 'one angry stomp'. The children must act out the adjective while making the sound. Discuss with the children what each of these sounded like: *was the 'angry stomp' loud? Were the 'lazy claps' slow? How did we make these sounds? For an angry stomp, we hit the ground hard with our feet. For lazy claps, we clapped slowly and dragged our hands apart.* Encourage the children to practise and expand their vocabulary by talking about each sound.

Activity: Action songs/rhymes

Popular songs such as 'Head, shoulders, knees and toes', 'Dingle dangle scarecrow' and 'Sleeping bunnies' encourage children to sing and use their body at the same time. Children explore movement, volume, pace and rhythm when engaging with songs and rhymes, both purely due to the song itself and also because of direction from an adult ('let's do it louder this time').

Aspect 4 – rhythm and rhyme

In Aspect 4, children are introduced to the rhythms and rhymes that can be heard in speech. This deeper awareness of speech and sounds supports children to engage in action rhymes and songs, anticipate what might come next in a pattern of sounds, build new vocabulary and begin to understand how words can be broken up into syllables. You may notice that we are getting closer and closer to being able to segment words later on: first in earlier aspects by discriminating between different sounds, and now by breaking words we hear up into syllables.

Activities for Aspect 4

Activity: Rhyming books – finish the rhyme

Using rhyming books is a fantastic way to introduce children to the world of rhyme. Rhyming often makes stories easier for children to engage with, as they follow a particular rhythm. Using a story children are familiar with, such as Julia Donaldson's *The Gruffalo* can encourage children to join in. Read a verse but stop before the last word of it, encouraging the children to finish the rhyme: 'A mouse took a stroll through the deep, dark wood. A fox saw the mouse, and the mouse looked ...'; pause to allow the children to finish the rhyme with 'good' (Donaldson and Scheffler, 1999). Continue this throughout the story, encouraging the children to join in and complete the rhymes. You can also discuss the rhyming words, noticing how words like 'lake' and 'snake' both have the 'ake' sound at the end.

Activity: Odd one out

Lay out some picture cards for the children. You may wish to start with just three or four cards. Each picture should rhyme with the others, apart from one. For example, you may have pictures of a cat, a bat, a hat and a fish. Say the words together and ask the children if any of the words sound alike. Some children may say that the cat, bat and fish are alike because they are all animals. Ensure to correct this misconception by telling the children that while they are all animals, we are listening to which words *sound* alike. Repeat the words several times. Discuss the sounds you can hear at the end of each word; 'cat and bat have the "at" sound. What other word has the "at" sound?' Keep repeating the words and encouraging the children to do the same, so they can both hear what they sound like and feel what their mouth does when saying each word. Once the odd one out has been found, start again with new cards. You may wish to focus on one word family, such as '-at' words, at first, before introducing more.

Activity: Clapping syllables

Have the children sit in a circle and each take a turn to say their name. Explain that we can break up names with claps. Give some examples, using the names of adults around you or toys in the room. Next, go around the circle again and support each child in clapping the syllables of their name. Then, ask all the children to do the same for that child's name. Continue doing this, going around the circle. Discuss the differences between names, such as some names only having one syllable (such as 'Luke'), or several names having the same number of syllables (such as 'Jess-i-ca' and 'Mo-ha-mud'). Using names makes this activity meaningful to the children. You can then introduce other words, by having objects in the middle of the circle that children can choose from.

Aspect 5: alliteration

For this aspect, focus shifts to the beginning of words, particularly their initial sounds. Being able to hear the initial sound in words is the very beginning of being able to segment them, continuing to build upon the skills we've explored so far in Phase One. Grouping words together based on their initial sound supports children to understand the make-up of words, explore how these words are similar or different when spoken and to understand alliteration.

Activities for Aspect 5

Activity: What's in my sound bag?

Focusing on one initial sound, fill a bag with items that begin with that phoneme. For example, for /c/ you might have a cat, comb, car, cow and cup. You wouldn't have objects such as a circle or celery as, although these words begin with the letter 'c', it makes the /s/ sound. Ask each child to pull something out of the bag and say its name. Concentrate on the initial sound of each object and how they all start with the /c/ sound. You can also play this game in reverse once children have a more solid understanding of initial sounds, by having a group of objects – some with different initial sounds – and asking the children which objects are allowed to go in the bag.

Activity: I spy

This one is an oldie but a goodie! This game involves the usual 'I spy with my little eye', but we use the letter sound rather than the letter name as the clue. For example, 'I spy with my little eye something beginning with /a/' (pronounced 'ah'). Children look to find something, such as an apple that starts with that sound. It is best to start this game by having a selection of objects to choose from, so the children have limited options and are not overwhelmed by the number of choices an entire room provides.

Activity: Alliterative sentences

Work with the children to make sentences that are as long as possible using alliteration. Give the children a subject to work with, for example 'snake'. Ask for words that also start with the 's' sound that we can use to describe our snake. This often turns into a very funny game! You may end up with a sentence such as *silly slithering smelly slow sausage snake.* Poor snake!

Aspect 6: voice sounds

This aspect focuses on exploring vocal sounds, understanding the differences in sounds we make when speaking and developing the skills of oral segmenting and blending. The way in which we use our voice changes depending on our mood, how urgently we need to relay information, when we need to be quiet or can be loud and a variety of other reasons. In this aspect we encourage children to explore how their voice changes and how they can make their voice change with their mouth shape, tongue placement and volume.

Activities for Aspect 6

Activity: Can you make your voice do this?

Playing with sounds our voices can make is a great way for children to explore their own voice and how they can change it. Give the children prompts, such as:

- hiss like a snake: sssss
- make an angry sound: arrghhh!
- what does your voice sound like when it's tired? Yawn
- be surprised: wow!
- moo like a cow: mooooo
- pretend you just heard a funny joke: laughing
- turn your voice into a bouncy ball: boing, boing, boing!
- make a noise like a donkey: ee-or
- be a doorbell: ding dong!

Of course, this isn't an exhaustive list, and you can also ask the children for their own ideas for more prompts!

Activity: Watch your sounds

Give the children some mirrors and ask them to watch their mouths as they make a sound. Discuss what happens when they make an 'oooo' sound (for example, 'my mouth turns into a circle'). Use different sounds to explore a range of mouth movements and tongue placements, from lips closed for /m/ to mouth wide open for /a/. In the outdoor area, use these mirrors to explore volume and what happens when we get louder or when we whisper. Give the children the opportunity to explore each sound and even share with each other, giving their peers ideas of sounds to make.

Activity: Whose voice is that?

Record either a group of adults or the children (ensure you have the relevant permission/consent to do so) when they are engaged in an activity and are talking about it. Play the recording to the children and ask whose voices they can hear. Can they hear their own voice? A friend's? What about when there are multiple voices at once? You can also play this game without recording and instead ask a group of children or adults to go behind a screen. Prompt one person at a time to speak and ask the other children in front of the screen if they can work out who was speaking. This helps to develop children's ability to tune into voice sounds and assign sounds to meaning (or in this case, voices to people).

Aspect 7: oral segmenting and blending

This aspect is all about listening to phonemes and remembering which order they happened in, to later blend those phonemes together and figure out the word they make. Being able to hear phonemes and blend them together will help children in Phase Two when they start to read the letter sounds and blend those together to visually read a word. For oral segmenting and blending, we are focusing on the sounds we hear, rather than trying to read them.

Activities for Aspect 7

Activity: Find the object

Have a group of objects for children to see. Ideally, the objects should be *CVC words*, meaning consonant–vowel–consonant. For example, a cat, bug, cup, dog, sock and pan. Sound out the name of one of the objects and see if the children can find the correct one. For example, if the adult sounds out /s/ o/ /ck/, can the children blend those sounds to realise they should pick up the sock? You may ask the children to repeat the sounds with you a few times until they can put them together and say the whole word.

Activity: Sound out and run

Have pictures or objects children can clearly see in different areas of the room or outdoor area. Again, these should be CVC words. When an adult sounds out the word, the children should run to the correct picture/object. Repeating this with the same words will help build children's confidence in their understanding of blending. If children run to different places, come together and sound out the word again, reminding the children that making mistakes is part of the game. When all the children can blend the word correctly, ask them to run together to the correct word. You can also encourage the children to work together, repeating the sounds the adult has said and helping each other to find the right picture/object.

Activity: I spy with segmenting

Back to an old favourite, we can change the I spy game to a segmenting version. Instead of the initial letter name or sound, we can play I spy by sounding out the word. For example, *I spy with my little eye, something with the sounds /k/ /e/ /t/ /l/ (kettle)*. As children become more confident in this game and their blending abilities, you can make the words a little more complex, containing more phonemes.

Revisiting Phase One

Some people reading this book may have skipped this chapter altogether, because they don't believe Phase One is important to know about when teaching children in Reception and above, but this is an enormous misconception. As educators, we need to know the foundations children have built in order to continue developing their skills appropriately. For this, we need to understand the components of that foundation. How does the learning they're approaching now build on what they already know? Are they prepared for this next stage of learning?

When reaching Phase Two and beyond, it's important to know the skills developed in Phase One in order to identify any gaps in learning that are hindering a child from moving forward. As educators we need to be able to not only recognise these signs, but also know how to address them, by going back to those Phase One aspects and filling in the gaps.

Signs of gaps in Phase One learning include:

- poor listening skills: cannot listen and attend for a short period of time, or differentiate between a variety of different sounds (always consider the possibility of a medical hearing problem when a child's listening or speaking skills are below the expected level for their age and stage of development);
- lacks the vocabulary needed to describe sounds they hear;
- unable to notice the initial sound in words;
- cannot recall sounds they have just heard: for example, if an adult says /c/ /u/ /p/, the child is unable to repeat those sounds;
- struggling to segment words they hear.

Not only is it vital to return to specific skills learnt in Phase One if a child has not developed such skills, it is also important to use Phase One aspects and activities alongside later phases (particularly Phase Two and Three). This will complement later learning and reminds us as educators that phonics phases are not strictly about learning in linear. If anything, remember that the teaching and learning in Phase One is extremely important for children's development *and* educators' own phonics knowledge.

Assessment

Throughout Phase One, practitioners will be observing and assessing children's development in order to plan future activities and next steps.

By the end of Phase One, children will be able to:

- distinguish between sounds in their environment;
- distinguish between speech sounds;
- orally blend and segment some words;
- recognise spoken words that rhyme (although this skill continues in the next phase, so children who cannot do this can still move onto Phase Two).

2
Phase Two

This chapter will cover:

1. what Phase Two involves;
2. the phonemes and graphemes covered in this phase;
3. how to introduce new phonemes and graphemes;
4. activities to support Phase Two learning;
5. segmenting and blending to read VC and CVC words;
6. tricky words covered in this phase;
7. Phase Two assessment.

Introduction

Phonics Phase Two is usually what comes to mind when people think about phonics; learning what letters look like (the grapheme), the sounds they make (the phoneme) and using this knowledge to decode words and read. Phase Two teaching in schools starts in Reception, with children usually learning a new letter sound almost every day. Typically, teachers will teach a new letter sound on Monday, Tuesday, Wednesday and Thursday, with Friday being the day to revise the sounds learnt. Some settings may take a different approach, teaching a new letter sound every day, or fewer sounds over a week. Whatever the structure, teachers usually aim to cover Phase Two during the first half term (or 'Autumn 1'). For schemes that do not follow the original *Letters and Sounds* (DfE, 2007) systematic synthetic phonics structure, the timeline may be different.

Introducing graphemes and phonemes

When introducing the graphemes, it is important to concentrate on lowercase letters (such as 'a' rather than 'A'), as these are what children will come across the most in their reading. Capital/uppercase letters can also be introduced alongside the lowercase, so children are exposed to both, but should not be the main focus. The same must be said for letter sounds and letter names, with sounds being the focus and the names being taught alongside them.

Many practitioners at the beginning of their career are surprised to learn that letter sounds are not taught in alphabetical order. Instead, they are taught in an order which allows children to read more words more quickly. There is also an argument that the order of the sounds gets progressively more difficult, and that earlier sounds are easier to pronounce than later sounds.

To demonstrate why we don't teach sounds in alphabetical order, let's take the first six letter sounds of the English alphabet and see how many CVC (Consonant-Vowel-Consonant) words we can make with them, compared to the first six letter sounds taught in systematic synthetic phonics. With these graphemes and their corresponding phonemes, we can make the following CVC words:

Table 2.1 Comparison of alphabetical order and SSP order

/a/ /b/ /c/ /d/ /e/ /f/	/s/ /a/ /t/ /p/ /i/ /n/
bad	at
bed	it
cab	in
dab	sat
dad	sit
fab	sap
fed	sit
	tap
	tan
	tip
	tin
	pat
	pan
	pit
	pin
	nap
	nip

Clearly, we can make many more words using this systematic synthetic phonics order of learning letter sounds. This allows children to practise segmenting and blending much earlier, with knowledge of only a few sounds.

Below is the order of sounds learnt in Phase Two, along with how to pronounce them. As we learnt in the previous chapter, pronouncing sounds correctly is paramount when teaching phonics. The *schwa* – adding the utterance 'uh' when it is not needed – must be avoided at all times. It can be helpful to listen to how sounds are pronounced rather than just reading them, which you can do on the Little Learners Education YouTube channel, @LittleLearnersVideos.

Set 1: s, a, t, p

Pronunciation:

/s/ such as in 'sun'

/a/ such as in 'apple'

/t/ such as in 'mat' – notice there is no 'uh' sound after the /t/

/p/ such as in 'spin' – again, there is no 'uh' after the /p/

Set 2: i, n, m, d

Pronunciation:

/i/ such as in 'ink'

/n/ such as in 'nap' – sounds like 'nnn' rather than 'nuh'

/m/ such as in 'man' – sounds like 'mmm' rather than 'muh'

/d/ such as in 'sad'

Set 3: g, o, c, k

Pronunciation:

/g/ such as in 'fig' – notice there is no 'uh' after the /g/ sound

/o/ such as in 'on'

/c/ and /k/ both make the same sound, such as in 'cook'

Set 4: ck, e, u, r

Pronunciation:

/ck/ makes the same sound as /c/ and /k/, such as in 'clock'

/e/ such as in 'egg'

/u/ such as in 'up'

/r/ such as in 'red' – sounds like 'rrr' rather than 'ruh'

Set 5: h, b, f, ff, l, ll, ss

Pronunciation:

/h/ such as in 'hill' – an unvoiced sound, meaning it should sound like breath escaping from your mouth, rather than 'huh'

/b/ such as in 'bell', with no 'uh' following it

/f/ and /ff/ are the same sound, such as in 'free' – sounds like 'fff' rather than 'fuh'

/l/ and /ll/ are the same sound, such as in 'hill' – sounds like 'lll' rather than 'luh'

/ss/ is the same sound as /s/, such as in 'hiss'

Activities for introducing new phonemes and graphemes

Activity: Tray game

Have one grapheme in the middle of a tray (can also be a table, a sheet of paper, etc.). Discuss the sound it makes. For this example, we will use /g/. Have lots of pictures or objects that start with /g/ in front of you, and a few that start with a different sound. Have the children look at each object and decide whether it can go in the tray. Discuss the initial sound of each object and if it matches the grapheme in the middle of the tray. Be sure to correct any misconceptions. For example, a child may think that the word 'three' starts with a /f/ sound (/f/ /r/ /ee/) because of incorrect pronunciation. You can also do this activity while working on fine motor skills, by having pictures children need to cut out and stick on a plate with the grapheme in the middle.

Activity: Objects in small-world play or role play

Consider the small-world and role-play areas in your setting. Could you incorporate your new sound into these? For example, when learning the /f/ sound, your small-world play could be a forest theme, with flowers and fairies. For /r/, you might have a rocket ship in the role-play area, with robots and lots of red objects.

Activity: Searching for sounds in messy play

For this game, use a Tuff tray™ or similar (a deeper tray can also be useful) and fill it with a messy play material, such as shaving foam (be mindful of allergies), sand, water, rice, soil or other natural resources. Hide either graphemes or objects beginning with specific sounds in the tray. Give children tools to search with or allow them to use their hands. When they find an object or grapheme, ask them to say what they have found and then to hide it again for their friends to find later. Ask the child what they know about the sound or grapheme and if they can think of words that start with the same initial sound.

Activity: Outdoor grapheme hunt

Put up large graphemes around the outdoor area – some up high, some lower. These graphemes should be those the children have already learnt. Give the children binoculars and ask them to go on a letter hunt. When they spot a grapheme, ask them what sound it makes. If a child or group of children is having trouble with a particular grapheme or sound, you can also play this game using just one grapheme and putting it up in multiple places. This allows using repetition in a fun way to support the child to learn that letter and sound.

Activity: Making graphemes with natural objects

Go outside with the children and collect natural resources (autumn is a handy time for this). Encourage the children to collect lots of dried leaves, acorns, conkers, pinecones, twigs, sticks, small stones and anything else they can find. Remind the children that we should not pick anything from plants; instead we should find objects that have already fallen. Once the children have collected their materials, they can use these to make the shape of a grapheme. You may wish to provide the children with templates for this or encourage them to work together to make one large letter.

How to teach a phonics session

Before introducing a new grapheme and phoneme, it is important to first revise any sounds already learnt. This doesn't have to take long – a simple flashcard game or letters on the board can be enough to both revise and assess whether any sounds need to be revisited.

Next, display the new grapheme and ask if anyone knows anything about this letter. Some children may know the letter name, or even its corresponding phoneme. Explain that this letter has a name *and* it makes a sound. While still showing the grapheme, encourage the children to make the sound with you. You can experiment with different ways to say the phoneme, such as loudly, quietly, fast and slow.

Show children some objects or pictures of things that start with that sound. For example, for /s/ you might show a sun, snake, slide and sweets. You wouldn't show a shoe, as although its first letter is 's', this begins with the /sh/ sound. You also wouldn't show a circle, as although this does start with the /s/ sound, it does not start with the 's' grapheme.

Ask the children if they can think of any other words that start with the sound. Is there anything around them that starts with /s/? Does anything they are wearing start with /s/? What about their toys at home – do any of those start with /s/? Show the children some objects or pictures of items that start with /s/. Ask them to repeat each word to practise saying and hearing /s/.

Depending on the scheme you use, there may be specific techniques to implement when introducing a sound. For example, *Jolly Phonics* uses an action and song (Jolly Learning, 1987); some have formation phrases for each grapheme, such as *'around the apple and down the leaf'* for 'a' (Miskin, 2002).

Next, practise writing the grapheme together. You can do this in the air with your finger, then on white boards once you have modelled how it is written. Some graphemes are harder than others to write; you may find that for 's', many children draw a wobbly vertical line, or that 'b', 'd' and 'p' often get confused. Children may also write graphemes upside down or in mirror-image (back to front). This is a natural part of a child's development and there is actually an evolutionary reason behind it. Our brains evolved to recognise objects and their mirror-image, so that if we see something from a different angle, we know it's still the same object. Being warned about a dangerous predator and knowing that it is still the same predator when it's walking in the other direction is crucial for survival (Hardach, 2023). The problem comes when the mirror-image of something takes on a new meaning, such as when 'b' is reversed and becomes 'd'. You can point out any errors when children mirror-write, but know that they will grow out of it (unless there is an underlying processing disorder present). Children are usually not even aware they have mirror-written until it is pointed out to them.

Moving on from writing the grapheme, children can start to segment and blend some CVC words, once they know a few sounds. Use words that start with the grapheme and phoneme you are currently learning, such as 'cat', 'cog', 'cot' and 'cap' for /c/. Model how we first break up the word by saying each individual phoneme and then blend those phonemes together to read the whole word.

Activities for specific sounds

Below are some ideas for activities that suit a particular letter sound.

Activity: The /s/ café

A café that only serves food starting with the /s/ sound, such as sausages, sandwiches, sweets, salad, soup, spaghetti, strawberries and so on. Have some of these items (real or toys, depending on your set-up) for children to play with and allow them to run their café. Children can visit, order food starting with /s/ and serve their friends. If a child asks for something that isn't already in the café's kitchen, the children can decide how to represent it with what they have, or draw/make something new (as long as it starts with /s/!). Make sure your /s/ café has lots of the 's' grapheme on show!

Activity: Popping bubbles for /p/

When learning the /p/ sound and grapheme, blowing and popping bubbles in the outdoor area gives children the opportunity to practise saying the /p/ sound each time they pop a bubble. You can even make 'bubble poppers', asking the children to use a range of materials to create a tool to pop bubbles. Encourage the children to decorate their bubble popper with pink and purple, and even with the grapheme 'p' if they can.

Activity: /m/ animals

Give the children the opportunity to make animal masks or ears on headbands – these can only be animals that start with /m/. These could include: monkey, mouse, moose, magpie, meerkat and macaw. Once the children have made their masks or headbands, ask them all to wear them and make the /m/ sound as they move around the room. When you give a signal (such as a bell ring), the children should ask the person next to them what animal they are and repeat that /m/ word.

Activity: /d/ digging for dinosaurs

Hide small dinosaur skeletons in a sandpit or tray of earth. Give the children tools to dig with, such as spades and spoons. Model what to do to find a dinosaur, by digging and saying 'dig, dig, dig!', encouraging the children to do the same. Among the dinosaur bones to be found, you may also want to bury the grapheme for /d/ by laminating some printed letters or using magnets or wooden letters you already have.

Activity: Glittery /g/

Have the 'g' grapheme for children to decorate using glue and the colours green, gold and grey. They can use glitter, as well as tissue paper, paint, crayons and other resources in these colours. Encourage the children to talk about the shape of the letter as well as the names of the colours they are using. Can they notice that they all begin with /g/?

Activity: /c/ caterpillar

Using a template for the grapheme, provide children with lots of resources to make their own caterpillar in the shape of a 'c'. Talk about the shape of the grapheme and how it curls round. You can even ask the children to give their caterpillar a name starting with /c/.

Activity: /r/ rocks

Using rocks in the outdoor area on a dry day, supply the children with paintbrushes and water. Model 'painting' an 'r' grapheme on a rock using the water and encourage the children to do the same, painting as many as they can. You can also observe what happens as the water begins to dry and even use the water to create 'rain' on the rocks.

Activity: /b/ buttons

Provide a range of buttons in different colours and sizes (be aware of choking hazards with small buttons). Ask the children to make the grapheme for /b/ using their buttons. You may wish to provide an outline for them to use or copy.

Activity: /f/ finding fairies

Hide some fairies (either toys or pictures) in the outdoor area. In addition, have some other items beginning with /f/ hidden for children to find, such as feathers, flowers and forks – these are items the fairies like to collect. Don't forget to also hide some 'f' graphemes too. Each time the children find an object or a fairy, encourage them to repeat its name and identify that it starts with the /f/ sound.

Segmenting and blending CVC words

In Phase One, children have learnt how to orally segment (break up a word into its phonemes) and blend (put the phonemes together to say the whole word). Segmenting and blending what they hear is still an important skill for children to continue developing in Phase Two. They also now have the graphemes to consider and move onto reading simple words using segmenting and blending. At this stage, we focus on CVC words. Some examples in Phase Two include:

- sat – /s/ /a/ /t/
- pin – /p/ /i/ /n/
- rock – /r/ /o/ /ck/
- huff – /h/ /u/ /ff/

It is now easier to see why we don't teach children the letter sounds in alphabetical order. With just Set 1, children know enough graphemes to try decoding (segmenting and blending) the words 'at', 'sat', 'pat', 'tap' and 'sap'. When introducing children to word reading, sticking to VC and CVC words allows children to practise decoding without becoming overwhelmed with too many phonemes. Reading words with adjacent consonants (such as 'flag' or 'milk') is a lot tricker. When reading, children must identify the grapheme, say its corresponding phoneme, retain the order in which they said those sounds and then blend them together to make a whole word – that's a lot of steps! Naturally, practising this skill with CVC words first is the most effective starting point.

Activities for CVC words

Below are some activities you can use with children who are learning to read CVC words. These can be adjusted to meet the individual needs of the children in your care.

Activity: Missing initial sound

Give children a picture of a CVC word, with the word written underneath but missing its initial sound. Can the children work out which sound is missing? Can they find the correct grapheme? Ask the children to then find other pictures of words that start with the same sound. When children become confident in this skill you can focus on multiple initial sounds, with children grouping the pictures together based on the sound they start with. Once children can identify initial sounds, you can play this game with the middle or last letter missing instead. This is a trickier skill, which may require a bit more support.

Activity: CVC puzzles

There are a range of CVC puzzles available to purchase, but you can also make your own. The puzzle should involve a picture and its CVC word. Separate the picture from the word and then separate the graphemes. Starting with a picture, children will need to find the correct graphemes and put them in order to make the word. By doing this, children are segmenting the word, recognising the graphemes and blending the sounds together to check they have created the correct word.

Activity: Word hunt

Hide a range of objects or pictures around the outdoor area for the children to find (again, these should be CVC words). Remind the children that we need to use our listening ears for this game! Segment the word and ask them to blend the sounds together to work out what the word is. When they have, they need to run around to find the object and bring it back to you. You can also add a timer to this game if the children are a bit more confident – just be mindful of any anxiety that certain children may have about feeling rushed or overwhelmed by the extra challenge. You can also provide the written words for children to choose from to match to the objects they have found.

Accents

Just when you think you've understood it all, we come to a bit of a hurdle: accents. There are myriad regional accents across the UK, as well as accents from other English-speaking countries and other accents influenced by a person's first language not being English. Accents can make many words sound different depending on who is pronouncing them. It should go without saying that children should not have to change the way they pronounce words due to their accent, as long as their pronunciation is consistent within their own accent. Twinkl Digest found that between 53 per cent and 61.7 per cent of teachers feel the need to change their accent when teaching phonics, due to reasons such as having a different accent to the region they are teaching in or even fearing prejudice from parents for their particular accent (Tayler, 2023).

Many words are pronounced differently in a variety of accents, but are still decodable no matter what accent they are being spoken in. For example, the /u/ sound in 'mug' may sound different in a London accent compared to a Yorkshire accent, but the word is still decodable for both.

Sometimes words differ in pronunciation so much that an accent changes whether a word is phonetically decodable. We typically see this in Phase Three and beyond, so will discuss this more in the next chapter.

Phase Two tricky words

Phase Two introduces *tricky words* or *common-exception words*, which are words that are not phonetically decodable. They are common exceptions to the usual phonics rules. For example, the word 'was' cannot be decoded as the 'a' is not making an /a/ sound but rather more of an /o/ sound. Similarly, words such as 'the', 'no' and 'he' cannot be phonetically decoded. Therefore, children learn these words by sight as they are not able to sound them out using their phonics knowledge. Some educators introduce these as having letters that are 'trying to trick us', because they are not making their usual sound. In this sense, tricky words are not named as such because they are difficult, but because they are *being* difficult! Children are taught these words alongside phonics, as many of these words are also *high-frequency words*, meaning they appear in texts very often, so children need to know how to read them. Different schemes may alter the words included in each phase.

List of Phase Two tricky words

the

go

no

to

into

Children are often also taught other high-frequency words together with these tricky words. These are words that can often be decoded, such as 'and' or 'mum', but appear so frequently in children's reading that it is beneficial for them to be able to read these words by sight, to help increase fluency when reading. Many settings refer to tricky words and high-frequency words together as *sight words*, but it is important for educators to remember that, in this case, not all sight words will be decodable.

Activities for tricky words

Below are some activities you can use to support children in learning tricky words. Learning these words involves a lot of repetition and rote learning, so fun and engaging activities are crucial when we teach them.

Activity: Tricky word hunt

Probably one of the more popular tricky word activities, this treasure-hunt style of game is always enjoyable. Using flashcards (purchased or homemade), scatter the tricky words around your environment. They can be hidden in toy boxes and pencil pots, or in the outdoor area stuck up on walls, trees and so on. You can amend the level of challenge in this game both by adjusting where the words are placed and which/how many words you choose to use. When the children find a word, they can bring it to you, read it and put it in the 'treasure chest' (a real chest or a simple box). To add even more challenge, you can provide a clue with each word that will help the children find the next one; this can be a written word or picture clue.

Activity: Matching tricky words

Using several pairs of flashcards, turn them over on a table. Children need to choose a card, turn it over and read the word. Then, they can choose another card, hoping to get the matching word. If they do find the match, they can keep the cards. If they don't, the cards are turned over again and the game continues. This game is great for developing children's skills of concentration, focus, memory and recall.

Activity: Finding tricky words in books

When reading with children, see if they can point out tricky words. You can do this when they read to you, when you read to them, or even just by opening a book and searching for the tricky words without reading the whole book. This helps children to recognise tricky words in a range of different fonts and sizes and is a way to make the repetition of learning tricky words a bit more interesting!

Activity: Feed the puppet

A firm favourite with young children! Use a puppet (bonus points if your puppet is a monster) and make sure you can control its mouth. Your puppet is very hungry, but only eats tricky words! Hold up a flashcard and ask the children to say the word. Only once they have read the word can the puppet 'eat' it. Make sure you add lots of silliness by making the puppet try to eat the card before it's been read and telling the puppet to stop being so cheeky or to be patient. This helps keep the children engaged as they laugh along and read the words to feed their new puppet friend.

Assessment

For children at this age and stage, practitioners use observation for continuous formative assessment of children and the skills they are developing.

When reaching the end of Phase Two, children should be able to:

- say the sound for every Phase Two letter/grapheme, with a secure understanding of s, a, t, p, i, n (the first graphemes and phonemes learnt);
- find the corresponding grapheme for any Phase Two sound;
- orally segment and blend CVC words;
- segment and blend to read VC words;
- spell (using magnetic or other tactile letters) VC words, such as 'as', 'if' or 'up';
- read all five Phase Two tricky words.

Some children will have mastered segmenting and blending CVC words at this point. For those who have not fully developed this skill yet, but know all of the Phase Two letter sounds, progressing onto Phase Three is still appropriate as segmenting and blending skills continue to be developed in the next phase.

Some children may be able to write letters with a pencil, some correctly formed. Most children should be able to 'write' the letters in the air, or in messy play like sand or shaving foam using their finger or a paintbrush. Children should be able to control a pencil well enough to write the letters l, t, i, h, n and m with reasonable accuracy.

Conclusion

Phase Two truly is an incredible phase to teach. When children first start this phase they cannot read. Perhaps they can recognise their name, or other words of personal significance, but they can't *read*. During Phase Two children quickly learn the skills they need to become readers. Being the adult who gets to give them this knowledge and then watch them progress is an absolute privilege. When a child starts to read to you for the first time, it is a moment you will always cherish, knowing that this is just the beginning of their reading journey.

3

Phase Three and Phase Four

This chapter will cover:

1. the skills learnt in Phase Three and Phase Four;
2. the graphemes and phonemes learnt in Phase Three;
3. digraphs and trigraphs;
4. activities to support Phase Three and Phase Four learning;
5. segmenting and blending to read CVCC, CCVC and polysyllabic words;
6. visual aids such as sound buttons and phoneme frames;
7. how accents can have an impact on phonics teaching and learning;
8. tricky words learnt in Phase Three and Phase Four;
9. writing;
10. assessment in Phase Three and Phase Four.

Introduction to Phase Three

When it comes to Phase Three, it is important to assess whether children are ready to move on from Phase Two before embarking on this next step in their phonics journey. Children should be able to recognise all (or most) Phase Two graphemes and say their corresponding sounds, be able to read some CVC words and read some tricky words. Children will continue to read more CVC words in Phase Three, as well as learning new graphemes and phonemes. Phase Three builds upon Phase Two by introducing new and more complex sounds, continuing to concentrate on *grapheme–phoneme correspondence* (GPC) and focusing on segmenting and blending skills using CVC words.

Digraphs and trigraphs

In Phase Three, children are introduced to *digraphs* and *trigraphs*. Don't worry if you've never heard of these words – most adults haven't! And yet, children of four or five years old are able to use these words with ease and in the correct context. Never be afraid to teach children the real word for something – it may seem complicated, but to the child, it's just another new word!

So, what are digraphs and trigraphs? Let us begin with the digraph: in short, this is a sound represented by two letters. For example, in the word 'chip', we have the digraph /ch/, represented by the letters 'c' and 'h'. Apart, these letters make their own individual sounds. When put together, they work as a team to make one sound: /ch/. Other examples of digraphs include /sh/ such as in 'ship' and /ai/ such as in 'nail'. When teaching children about digraphs, we usually use the phrase: 'two letters, one sound', using our fingers to show two and one respectively. Children can continue to repeat this phrase and corresponding actions each time they are introduced to a new digraph, or when revising those they have learnt. This can help to reinforce that knowledge. When studying digraphs we can put them into two categories: consonant digraphs and vowel digraphs. As the names suggest, consonant digraphs are made up only of consonants, such as /ch/ or /sh/, and vowel digraphs are made up only of vowels, such as /ai/ or /ee/. We will look closer at each of these digraphs, along with others and their pronunciations, later in this chapter.

Now we know that a digraph is two letters making one sound, we can move onto the trigraph. Unsurprisingly, the trigraph is a sound represented by three letters. For example, in the word 'night' we have the trigraph /igh/, represented by 'i', 'g' and 'h'. Together, these letters make just one sound: /igh/. Other examples of trigraphs include /air/ such as in 'chair' and /ear/ such as in 'fear'.

Phase Three sounds

Below is a list of the Phase Three sounds, the order they are taught in and their pronunciations. Remember, you can also listen to how each of these sounds are pronounced by visiting youtube.com/@LittleLearnersVideos.

Set 6: j, v, w, x
Pronunciation:
/j/ such as in 'jug'
/v/ such as in 'van'
/w/ such as in 'web'
/x/ such as in 'box'

Set 7: y, z, zz, qu
Pronunciation:
/y/ such as in 'yak'
/z/ and /zz/ make the same sound, such as in 'zip' and 'fizz'
/qu/ such as in 'queen'

Set 8: ch, sh, th, *th*, ng
Pronunciation:
/ch/ such as in 'chat'
/sh/ such as in 'ship'
/th/ such as in 'thin' – /th/ is the unvoiced version on this digraph
/*th*/ such as in 'this' – /*th*/ is the voiced version of this digraph, often shown using italics when teaching to differentiate between the unvoiced and voiced sounds represented by 'th'
/ng/ such as in 'swing'

Set 9: ai, ee, igh, oa, oo, *oo*, ar, or, ur, ow, oi, ear, air, ure, er
Pronunciation:
/ai/ such as in 'rain'
/ee/ such as in 'three'
/igh/ such as in 'night'
/oa/ such as in 'goat'
/oo/ such as in 'moon' – /oo/ is the long sound for this digraph

/oo/ such as in 'book' – /oo/ is the short sound for this digraph, often represented using italics when teaching to differentiate it from the long /oo/ sound

/ar/ such as in 'car'

/or/ such as in 'born'

/ur/ such as in 'fur'

/ow/ such as in 'cow'

/oi/ such as in 'coin'

/ear/ such as in 'beard'

/air/ such as in 'hair'

/ure/ such as in 'pure'

/er/ such as in 'fern'

Introducing digraphs and trigraphs

When introducing digraphs, it can be helpful to use the actual word 'digraph'. Children are learning so many new words at this stage, so even if the word sounds complicated, they will usually handle it with the ease of any other word they have learnt.

Explain to the children that you will be showing them a special kind of sound today. Tell them the name, digraph, and ask them to repeat it a few times. Explain that a digraph is a sound that has two letters – how exciting! Show the children the first digraph grapheme: 'ch'. Ask them what they see. Children will usually say they see /c/ and /h/, which would be correct for them at this point in their learning. Tell the children that, yes, when they are working alone these letters do make those sounds, but when they are together they make a new sound, /ch/. Ask the children to repeat the sound, experimenting with different ways of saying it (loud, quiet, fast, slow).

Show the children some pictures or objects that start with this sound. It is best to first introduce this new sound as an initial sound, like in 'chip', and move onto words like 'lunch' at a later time. Ask the children to say the word for every picture or object, and practise saying the /ch/ sound again. Ask the children if they can think of any other words that start with the same sound. Practise segmenting and blending CVC words that contain this digraph. Be sure to correct any misconceptions at this stage; for /ch/, many children will assume words starting with 'tr' such as 'tree' and 'train' begin with the /ch/ sound because of mispronunciation.

Sound buttons

Using *sound buttons* can be very helpful at this stage. Sound buttons are dots and lines used to show whether a sound in a word is represented by one or more letters. For single grapheme sounds, we use a dot. For digraphs and trigraphs, we use lines. This allows children to clearly see how many phonemes are in a word and which graphemes are representing them. See the examples below:

cat

ship

church

Phoneme frames

We can also use *phoneme frames* to help children segment words into their phonemes. Similar to sound buttons, phoneme frames help children to see how many phonemes are in a word and which graphemes represent them. Each phoneme is separated in a table, as shown in Figure 3.1.

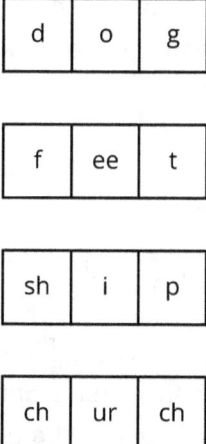

Figure 3.1 Phonemes

Some phoneme frames also give a visual clue about what grapheme will 'fit', by using different-sized boxes. This can be useful when children are writing a word (see Figure 3.2).

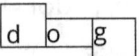

Figure 3.2   Example of a phoneme frame with a visual cue

CVC words with digraphs

In Phase Three, we are still concentrating on segmenting and blending CVC words. However, once digraphs and trigraphs are added into the mix, things can become a little more complicated. Until now, children have been used to segmenting by saying a sound for every letter in a word. For example, the word 'cat', on the one hand, is made up of three letters and three graphemes and phonemes: /c/ /a/ /t/. The word 'chip', on the other hand, contains four letters but just three graphemes and phonemes: /ch/ /i/ /p/. The word 'night' contains five letters but just three graphemes and phonemes: /n/ /igh/ /t/. When practising to read with digraphs and trigraphs, the most common misconception we see is children reading by segmenting the grapheme, for example /c/ /h/ /i/ /p/ for 'chip'. This of course makes it near-impossible to blend the sounds together to correctly read the word. Sound buttons can help with this misconception and assist children in recognising a two-letter or three-letter grapheme when it is in a word.

Middle and end sounds

Children will have been developing their understanding of recognising initial sounds up until this point. Now, children can move onto recognising the middle and end sounds of words. This is a more difficult skill. When learning the sound /x/, children will mostly be seeing this sound at the end of words, so will be practising recognising the end sound frequently. Being able to segment and remember the order sounds appear in is a tricky skill and it may take some time – children often (but not always) find it easier to identify the end sound in words compared to the middle sound(s).

Activities for Phase Three

Below are some activity ideas for Phase Three provision. The activities from the previous chapter can also be used and adjusted to meet the needs of where children are in their phonics learning.

Activity: Matching digraphs

A simple game that involves pairs of digraph flashcards. For example, you may have two 'ai' cards, two 'ch' cards and two 'sh' cards. Place the cards upside down and ask the children to turn them over two at a time, trying to find the matching pair. This allows for children to focus on recognising the grapheme, its shape and the letters used in it. Once a pair has been found, practise saying the sound together before removing those cards from the game. You can add more cards and graphemes as children learn new digraphs and become more confident in recognising them.

Activity: Digraph treasure

Place a treasure box in the middle of a table or tray, with a digraph written or stuck on it. Tell the children that the pirates have lost all of their treasure and need help to find it. However, these pirates like to make sure they only collect treasure with a particular sound – for this example, let's use /sh/. Place items around the table (or entire setting, depending on how much space you want to use for the game) that contain the /sh/ sound. This may include shark, ship, shoes, shells, fish, brush, etc. Also include some items that do not contain that sound. The children must identify which items belong in the treasure chest and put them inside. Once they have put all of the items inside, check them together, saying each word aloud and focusing on the digraph. You may even wish to then leave the treasure chest outside, telling the children that the pirates will collect their treasure at nighttime and leave a new treasure chest (with a new grapheme) for them to find in the morning.

Activity: Playdough sound buttons

Using playdough, show the children how they can make their own sound buttons. Prepare CVC words using the sounds the children have learnt and laminate them so they can be used multiple times. Using the playdough, place a small ball under single letter sounds and a line under digraphs (you might even refer to these as beans and sausages). Encourage the children to work out if they need a dot or line (or bean or sausage!) under a grapheme. When they have placed their sound buttons, they can use a finger to squash them as they read each sound. The aim of this activity is to be able to segment words, particularly those containing digraphs.

Activity: Fishing for digraphs

In the water tray, place objects such as toy fish or building blocks that have digraphs written on each of them. You may wish to add soap to make a bubbly surface (just be mindful of allergies). Provide children with nets and ask them to fish out the objects and read the digraph written on each of them. Once they have, they can place the item in a bucket and continue 'fishing'. Once they have completed the activity, ask the children to put the items back into the water so their peers can have a go.

Activity: Duplo™ CVC words

Build words using Duplo bricks. Use one long brick and write the word on it. Next, use a 1x1 brick to write each single letter grapheme on and 2x1 bricks for digraphs. Ask the children to find the correct graphemes and build the word on top of the long brick. They can then take this apart and use the same bricks, along with others, to build more words you have prepared. Children should also be encouraged to make their own words if they feel confident to do so.

Accents

In the previous chapter, we learnt that accents can affect the way we teach and learn phonics. Depending on where you teach, the accents of the children you teach, and indeed your own accent, words can sound remarkably different. In Phase Two, we saw that words can be pronounced differently but still remain decodable in a range of accents. However, in Phase Three we begin to notice the big differences accents can make, to the extent that some words become decodable – or non-decodable – depending on the accent used.

For example, in a typical South English accent, the word 'bath' is not decodable. The 'a' is not making the /a/ sound, but rather more of an /ar/ sound; it is pronounced /b/ /ar/ /th/. Say this word with a more Northern English accent, though, and it may just become decodable. A person from Yorkshire may pronounce bath with the /a/ sound: /b/ /a/ /th/. Thus, the word becomes decodable. This is the case for many words when we look at accents from the South of England compared with the North. This is not the case for all accents in these regions, of course, but we can see a stark contrast between the decodability of words when we compare these accents. Many American accents also use the short /a/ sound in words just as many Northern English accents do.

There are also differences in pronunciation that result in certain words rhyming in one accent but not in another accent. In England, the words 'foot' and 'cut' rhyme for '82% of northern speakers, 48% of speakers in the Midlands, and just 6% of southern speakers' (MacKenzie et al., 2016).

Phase Three tricky words

Phase Three brings with it a new set of tricky words. As a quick reminder, tricky words are common-exception words (they cannot be decoded using a child's phonics knowledge) which children need to learn 'by sight'. They are often also high-frequency words, so learning to recognise them by sight is helpful for fluent reading.

List of Phase Three tricky words

- he
- she
- we
- me
- be

was

my

you

her

they

all

are

Activities for tricky words

The tricky word activities from Phase Two can be used again for these new tricky words. Below are a few more activities you can try alongside them.

Activity: Splat the tricky word

Place tricky words on the floor, large enough for the children to read easily. Give the children fly swats (or something similar) and tell them to 'splat' the word when you call it out. Children can also take turns at calling out each tricky word for their friends. You can call out each tricky word once, or keep going back to a particular word if children are finding it particularly tricky to recognise. Differentiate this activity by reducing or increasing the number of tricky words you include.

Activity: Spot and dot

On an A4 piece of paper (or larger), write a tricky word in the centre in large letters. This is our 'target word'. Around the target word should be other smaller tricky words, repeated around the page, as well as smaller versions of the target word. Children can dip their fingers in paint and 'dot' the target tricky word each time they see it. You can do this as a laminated sheet so it can be reused, or print enough for all children to have their own. This activity helps children to recognise the shape of the word, the letters used to make it and uses repetition in a fun and engaging way.

Activity: Tricky words in books

This game involves looking at a tricky word and then trying to find it in a book. Children can look through as many books as they need to until they find the word. Once they have shown you, they are given the next tricky word to find. Once children have found all of the tricky words provided, they win the game. To differentiate, you may wish to focus on only finding one tricky word multiple times, allowing children to work in teams or adding adult support when searching.

Assessment

Ongoing formative assessment allows practitioners to monitor the progress of children and identify misconceptions along the way. More summative assessment can be undertaken, but should not be too extensive as children are still young and respond best to engaging, play-based learning.

When reaching the end of Phase Three, children should be able to:

- say the corresponding sound for all (or most) of the Phase Two and Phase Three graphemes;
- identify the corresponding grapheme when they have heard a phoneme learnt in Phase Two and Phase Three;
- segment and blend to read CVC words that are comprised of Phase Two and Phase Three graphemes;
- read all (or most) of the tricky words learnt in Phase Two and Phase Three;
- write phonetically plausible CVC words, spelling them in line with their own knowledge of phonics and the graphemes learnt thus far;
- write the tricky words 'the', 'to', 'I', 'no' and 'go' with correct spelling;
- write each letter correctly, even if they are using an example (such as from a letter mat) to copy from.

Introduction to Phase Four

During Phase Four, no new phonemes or graphemes are introduced. By now, children will have learnt all 44 (sometimes referred to as 42, depending on accent) phonemes and their corresponding graphemes and be able to read CVC words using single letter graphemes, digraphs and trigraphs. They will be able to read some tricky words and will also be able to write words based on their phonetic knowledge.

Phase Four focuses on increasing fluency in reading, as well as reading more complicated words, such as those with adjacent consonants and polysyllabic words (words with more than one syllable). In this phase, we will see the terms 'CVCC' and 'CCVC', showing where the adjacent consonants are in the word.

Examples of *CVCC words* include:

pink

tent

chomp

toast

Examples of *CCVC words* include:

slug

grin

crash

flight

Reading words with adjacent consonants can be difficult at first. Children may segment a word, then blend the sounds together, but drop one of the sounds. For example, 'slug' becomes 'lug' and 'milk' becomes 'mil' or 'ilk'. As children practise this skill they will become more confident and be able to read even more complex words. When a child is 'dropping' a sound, encourage them to go back to the beginning of the word and try again. Be encouraging, telling them, 'You almost got it!' and help by segmenting the word for the child to hear, so they can identify the sound missed when blending.

Activities for CCVC and CVCC words

Activity: Listen and frame

Using voice recorders like Talking Tins™, record one CCVC or CVCC word per device. Provide the children with phoneme frames that have four boxes. Allow them to listen to the recorded word as many times as they need to and ask them to write the sounds they can hear, breaking them up into the frame. The children will see that there should be four sounds, which can help as a visual cue if they are struggling to move from CVC words to adjacent consonants. To differentiate for children who are still learning to write graphemes, you may also provide the graphemes on laminated cards or tiles for the children to use. Once they have put the graphemes in their phoneme frame, ask the child to sound out the word they have made and decide if it matches the word they heard.

Activity: Word fix

Provide pictures of CVCC or CCVC words. For example, these may include 'nest', 'milk', 'sand' and 'crab'. Underneath each picture should be the written word with one grapheme missing. This can be an initial or end consonant, or even a middle vowel, depending on which skill children are working on. Children need to 'fix' the word by identifying the missing sound and selecting the correct grapheme to represent it. Once the grapheme is in place (either by writing, sticking or placing it) children can blend the sounds together to check that they have created the correct word.

> ### Activity: Giant chalk words
>
> In the outdoor area, use chalk to write CVCC or CCVC words on the ground. These should be large enough for the children to jump on each grapheme. You can also add sound buttons or a phoneme frame if you wish. Children can take it in turns to jump on each grapheme, saying the corresponding phoneme. Children can do this one at a time or in groups of four, with each child being responsible for one grapheme. Once the sounds have been said (or shouted!) in order, the children can work together to blend the sounds together and read the full word.

Polysyllabic words

While the example words in this chapter thus far are still monosyllabic, children will come across words with multiple syllables in this phase. These words, known as *polysyllabic* words, add another challenge to reading. Not only do children now need to contend with multiple phonemes, digraphs, trigraphs and adjacent consonants, but they now also need to be able to recall all of the sounds in a much longer word.

Examples of polysyllabic words include:

children – two syllables

swimming – two syllables

banana – three syllables

electrical – four syllables

Many polysyllabic words are also *compound words*, which are created when two or more individual words come together to make a new word with its own meaning. Examples of compound words include:

raincoat = rain + coat

toothbrush = tooth + brush

jellyfish = jelly + fish

When reading these words, it can be helpful for children to break them up (sometimes known as 'chunking' or 'chunk it up'), segmenting and blending the first 'word', then the second and then bringing them together. For example:

toothbrush: /t/ /oo/ /th/ 'tooth' + /b/ /r/ /u/ sh/ 'brush' = toothbrush

The compound words above are known as *closed* compound words, as there is no space between them. There are also *open* compound words, such as 'living room' or 'frying pan', which are still represented by two separate words, but when those words are used together they take on a new meaning. Children may also come across hyphenated compound words, usually when being used as an adjective to describe a noun, such as 'long-lasting glue'.

Writing

At this stage, children will be getting more confident with writing in a phonetically plausible way – that is, writing in the way words sound, rather than using their correct spelling. Once children have reached Phase Four, they will know how to spell some common-exception words correctly, as well as some high-frequency words. The emphasis on spelling increases now, with many children focusing on spelling practice and spelling tests in school. Spelling can prove to be difficult for many children due to the myriad of complexities in the English language when it comes to how words are spelt; many 'rules' do not apply for some words as they do for others. One reason for this discrepancy is that the English language has been influenced by other languages throughout its lifetime, with many words we use today having come from other countries. Children will focus on spelling CVC, CVCC and CCVC words at this stage.

Assessment

During Phase Four, it is imperative to undertake ongoing formative assessment to identify any misconceptions that have stuck around from previous phases. These misconceptions need to be addressed before children are able to confidently take on Phase Four learning. Support should be given to children at the level they are currently working at. Too often children are dragged through the phonics phases as if they are nets that will just scoop up the knowledge somehow.

Even during Phase Four, which usually takes place during Year 1 at school, children still respond well to engaging and play-based learning. It is important to remember this as a summative assessment that is too formal at this stage can hinder a child's ability to show how much they actually know. With this in mind, misconceptions during Phase Four learning should also be identified and managed appropriately.

When reaching the end of Phase Four, children should be able to:

- say the corresponding sound for all of the Phase Two and Phase Three graphemes;
- identify the corresponding grapheme when they have heard a phoneme learnt in Phase Two and Phase Three;
- segment and blend to read words containing adjacent consonants (such as CVCC and CCVC words);
- read the tricky words learnt thus far;
- segment words containing adjacent consonants in order to spell them;
- spell the tricky words 'he', 'she', 'we', 'me', 'be', 'was', 'my', 'you', 'her', 'they', 'all' and 'are';
- write each letter independently, usually forming them correctly.

Conclusion

Phase Three and Phase Four involve a lot of new skills, graphemes, phonemes and concepts for children to understand. From digraphs and trigraphs to reading polysyllabic words and understanding suffixes, these two phases can feel overwhelming at times. However, using the systematic approach to phonics that SSP offers allows children to develop each skill in a structured way, ensuring that they have a good understanding of each skill before moving on. Children will begin to read a much wider range of texts which can be exciting! Using visual cues like sound buttons and phoneme frames can help to develop children's writing and give them even more independence.

4
Phase Five and Phase Six

This chapter will cover:

1. the skills learnt in Phase Five and Phase Six;
2. split digraphs;
3. alternative pronunciations and spellings;
4. activities to support learning in Phase Five and Phase Six;
5. how accents can impact learning at this stage;
6. past tense and suffixes;
7. writing and spelling;
8. comprehension;
9. assessment for Phase Five and Phase Six.

Introduction to Phase Five

When children reach Phase Five, they will be able to decode and read CVC words, words with adjacent consonants and even some polysyllabic words. They can also read a wider variety of common-exception (tricky) words, write some of these and write letters with increasing accuracy. Children have begun writing words with correct spelling, rather than solely relying on their phonetic knowledge to spell. In Phase Five, the true nature of how complex the English language is becomes much more apparent; it 'features grammatical rules that are often broken … and spelling and pronunciation irregularities that perplex even native speakers' (Propio, 2023).

Phase Five brings with it a new phoneme, new graphemes, alternative spellings for known phonemes, a new type of digraph and more tricky words.

Phase Five phonemes and graphemes

Children will learn a new phoneme in Phase Five: /zh/ (sometimes represented as /zch/). This sound can be heard in words such as 'measure', 'vision' and 'beige'. The reason some words contain the /zh/ sound usually has to do with the letters' relationship with each other. We see this sound most commonly with words containing 'sure', 'sion' and 'ge'. This is not an exhaustive list and many words using the /zh/ phoneme have been influenced by or taken from other languages, such as in the word 'beige', the etymology of which is French (*Online Etymology Dictionary*, n.d.).

Phase Five also introduces some new graphemes, which each represent a phoneme children have learnt before:

- 'ay' such as in 'play'
- 'ou' such as in 'out'
- 'ie' such as in 'pie'
- 'ea' such as in 'eat'
- 'oy' such as in 'boy'
- 'ir' such as in 'girl'
- 'ue' such as in 'glue'
- 'aw' such as in 'paw'
- 'wh' such as in 'when'
- 'ph' such as in 'elephant'
- 'ew' such as in 'flew'
- 'oe' such as in 'toe'
- 'au' such as in 'launch'
- 'a_e' such as in 'cake'
- 'e_e' such as in 'eve'
- 'i_e' such as in 'five'
- 'o_e' such as in 'home'
- 'u_e' such as in 'cube'

The final five graphemes in this list are known as *split digraphs*. You may, however, be more familiar with the *magic e*, a term referring to the same type of grapheme. Some settings have decided in more recent years to stop using the term 'magic e' as it does not accurately explain the relationship between the 'e' and the vowel it is working with. However, many practitioners still use the term and also use it interchangeably with split digraph. It is therefore helpful to know both terms.

Split digraph

A split digraph is a sound made with two letters – much like a regular digraph – which is split in the middle by another consonant. The two letters – a vowel and an 'e' – work together to make a single sound. The idea of a magic e focuses on recognising that if a word ends in 'e', it may be changing the vowel that came before it. We sometimes teach this as the 'e' making the vowel 'say its name', which means the 'e' at the end signifies that the vowel will change from a short vowel sound to a long vowel sound. However, some practitioners dislike this explanation as the 'e' isn't changing anything, it is simply working together with the vowel to make a new sound.

When using sound buttons, split digraphs use a different type of symbol than the dots and lines we have used so far. Instead, a swooping line connects the two. Below are some examples:

bake

eye

mile

cone

tube

This swooping line symbol shows that the two letters are connected, working together to make one sound. Therefore, children say the vowel sound represented and then do not need to pronounce the 'e' at the end, as it has already been used as part of the split digraph.

Alternative spellings

Phase Five introduces alternative spellings for phonemes children already know. There are many ways to write certain sounds; for example, children will know the /ai/ sound represented by 'ai' as in 'tail', but will now learn that this sound can be represented by 'ay' as in 'play' and 'ey' as in 'grey'. Many words that were trickier in earlier phases will become decodable in Phase Five.

Below are examples of alternative spellings for a wide range of phonemes:

Known phoneme and grapheme: /e/ such as in 'bed'
Alternative spellings:
'ea' such as in 'bread'

Known phoneme and grapheme: /i/ such as in 'bin'
Alternative spellings:
'y' such as in 'myth'

Known phoneme and grapheme: /u/ such as in 'cup'
Alternative spellings:
'o' such as in 'brother'
'ou' such as in 'double'

Known phoneme and grapheme: /ar/ such as in 'car'
Alternative spellings:

'al' such as in 'half' (dependent on accent)
'a' such as in 'bath' (dependent on accent)

Known phoneme and grapheme: /oi/ such as in 'foil'
Alternative spellings:
'oy' such as in 'boy'

Known phoneme and grapheme: /ai/ such as in 'rain'
Alternative spellings:
'ay' such as in 'play'
'ey' such as in 'grey'
'ei' such as in 'vein'
'eigh' such as in 'eight' (this is a quadgraph: four letters making one sound)
'a_e' such as in 'same'

Known phoneme and grapheme: /ee/ such as in 'green'
Alternative spellings:
'y' such as in 'funny' (many children will learn this in an earlier phase, due to how common it is)
'ey' such as in 'key'
'ea' such as in 'bead'
'ie' such as in 'chief'
'e_e' such as in 'even'

Known phoneme and grapheme: /igh/ such as in 'night'
Alternative spellings:
'i' such as in 'lion'
'ie' such as in 'pie'
'y' such as in 'try'
'i_e' such as in 'five'

Known phoneme and grapheme: /oa/ such as in 'goat'
Alternative spellings:
'ow' such as in 'snow'
'oe' such as in 'toe'
'o' such as in 'no'
'o_e' such as in 'nose'

Known phoneme and grapheme: /oo/ such as in 'spoon'
Alternative spellings:
'ew' such as in 'flew'
'ui' such as in 'fruit'
'ue' such as in 'glue'

Known phoneme and grapheme: /oo/ such as in 'book'
Alternative spellings:
'oul' such as in 'could'

Known phoneme and grapheme: /f/ such as in 'fish'
Alternative spellings:
'ph' such as in 'elephant'

Known phoneme and grapheme: /j/ such as in 'jam'
Alternative spellings:
'g' such as in 'giraffe'
'dge' such as in 'badge'

Known phoneme and grapheme: /w/ such as in 'wet'
Alternative spellings:
'wh' such as in 'when'

Known phoneme and grapheme: /n/ such as in 'not'
Alternative spellings:
'gn' such as in 'gnome'
'kn' such as in 'knock'

Known phoneme and grapheme: /sh/ such as in 'ship'
Alternative spellings:
'ch' such as in 'chef'
't(ion)' such as in 'nation'

Known phoneme and grapheme: /s/ such as in 'sit'
Alternative spellings:
'c' such as in 'face', 'mice' and 'cyan'

Known phoneme and grapheme: /or/ such as in 'corn'
Alternative spellings:
'aw' such as in 'prawn'
'au' such as in 'audio'
'al' such as in 'talk'
'our' such as in 'tour' (depending on accent)

Known phoneme and grapheme: /ear/ such as in 'fear'
Alternative spellings:
'ere' such as in 'here'
'eer' such as in 'cheer'

Known phoneme and grapheme: /air/ such as in 'hair'
Alternative spellings:
'are' such as in 'care'
'ear' such as in 'bear'

Yes, we're all thinking the same thing: it's a wonder any of us learnt to read at all!

Alternative pronunciations

As well as alternative spellings for sounds they already know, children will also learn that there are different pronunciations for graphemes they already know. We can see this in the list above – for example, with the grapheme 'ow' making the /ow/ sound in 'cow' and the /oa/ sound in 'snow'. Another example is the grapheme 'ea', making the /ee/ sound in 'bead' and the /e/ sound in 'bread'. This can naturally be quite confusing when coming across words that share the same grapheme but are pronounced in different ways. Earlier in Phase Three, children were introduced to the digraphs 'oo' and 'th', which each have two slightly different pronunciations. Now though, there are far more graphemes like this to contend with. Grapheme and phoneme mats (mats with each grapheme and examples of what sounds it can make, or each phoneme and examples of graphemes it can be represented by) can be extremely helpful at this stage. As children come across new words, they may need to try segmenting using a few different phonemes for the same grapheme until they get it right. For example, a child may see the word 'sky' and sound it out three times: /s/ /k/ /y/, which would not blend to make a word, /s/ /k/ /ee/, which would blend to make a plausible word but not the correct word for this spelling and, finally, /s/ /k/ /igh/, blending to read the correct word. As children continue to develop their fluency in reading, they will begin to learn many more words by sight, eventually needing to sound them out less and less.

Activities for Phase Five

Many of the activities from previous phases can be adjusted and used in Phase Five. Below are some more Phase Five-specific activities.

Activity: Phoneme finder

Read a text to the children, making sure they have a copy of it as well. On the first read-through, ask the children to simply listen. On the second read-through, ask the children to listen out for a particular phoneme, such as /ai/. Each time they hear a word with this sound, repeat the word together and underline it. Remember: for this activity we are focusing on hearing the phoneme, not finding a particular grapheme. Keep doing this until you reach the end of the text, and then go through the words together. Write each word where the children can see them and discuss the different spellings. For example, you may have the words 'rain', 'plain', 'same', 'cake', 'play' and 'day'. Create a table with each different /ai/ grapheme you have found at the top, and ask the children to put each word in the right place. Discuss how, even though the sound is spelt differently in these words, all of them still contain the /ai/ sound. You can repeat this activity each day, focusing on the same phoneme for a few days or a different phoneme each day.

Activity: Rare spellings

Show children a table based on one phoneme that shows all of its potential graphemes. For this example, we will use the /oo/ phoneme. At the top of the table, list each common possible grapheme for this sound: 'oo', 'ue', 'ui', 'ew' and 'u_e'. List words under these headings, showing that some graphemes are more common for this sound than others. At the end of the table, list the 'rare' graphemes for this sound, such as 'o' in 'tomb', 'ou' in 'group' and 'u' in 'truth'. Explain that some spellings are much more rare than others and that we can use this knowledge when we write words to give us the best chance of spelling them correctly. Ask children to think of more words that contain the /oo/ sound and ask them which grapheme is needed when spelling it. Ask children to write down the words they think of. If misconceptions occur, such as using the incorrect grapheme, now is the time to correct these and help children learn the correct spelling of a word. Tell the children that in this activity we are bound to get things wrong because there are so many graphemes to choose from. The aim of this activity is to find out the correct spelling using the clues the table gives us rather than knowing them all already!

Activity: Phonics peg wheel

Divide a paper plate into several sections using lines. The number of sections will depend on how many phonemes you would like to focus on. In each section, write a known grapheme for a particular phoneme. In this example, we have divided our plate into five

(Continued)

sections and have written 'ai', 'ee', 'igh', 'oa' and 'oo' on them. Next, write the alternative graphemes for these sounds on pegs. Children can then look through all of the pegs and attach them to the correct section of the paper plate. For example, the peg with 'eigh' written on it would be attached to the 'ai' section of the plate because the graphemes represent the same phoneme. Children can make their own peg wheels or you can provide enough in your provision for children to take turns using. This activity allows children to explore each phoneme and the graphemes that can be used to spell it, further consolidating that knowledge by grouping the graphemes together by phoneme.

Activity: Grapheme clock

In the outdoor area, draw a large circle on the ground with chalk. Write 12 graphemes around the inside, like numbers on a clock. There should be two graphemes for each phoneme. For example, you could use 'ai', 'ay', 'ee', 'ea', 'igh', 'ie', 'oa', 'oe', 'oo', 'ue', 'oi' and 'oy'. Mix the graphemes up so they are not next to their 'partner' on the clock. Children take turns standing in the middle. When you call out a phoneme, the child must use their arms like the hands of a clock to point at the two graphemes that make that sound. Children can also call out phonemes for their peers, making the game more independent.

Activity: The 'magic e' game

If your setting uses the term 'magic e', this can be a fun activity to show how words change when the magic e works together with a vowel to make a new sound. Provide lots of CVC words on cards for the children to read. Also supply an 'e' card for them to use – you may even wish to stick the 'e' on the end of a wand to make it more magical, or make magic e wands with the children first. Ask the child to choose a CVC word and read it. Then, add the magic e on the end and read the word again, remembering that we now have a split digraph in the word. Ask how the sound has changed and what word we now have. You may decide to use only CVC words that will still be real words when the e is added, or include some CVC words that will turn into nonsense words when the e is added, giving the activity an extra level of challenge.

Activity: Mirror words

Write words on cards using the known graphemes from Phase Two and Phase Three. Next, write more cards, but this time using some of the new alternative graphemes learnt in Phase Five. These alternative grapheme cards should be written in mirror image. When children try to read the words, they will need to hold the alternative grapheme card in front of a mirror in order to read it. This game is a fun and engaging way to highlight the alternative spellings being taught in Phase Five.

Accents

As we learnt in the previous chapter, accents can change whether or not a word is decodable. In Phase Five, we also notice that different accents can change whether or not a phoneme is represented by a particular spelling. For example, in a South English accent, the graphemes 'ee' and 'y' can both make the /ee/ sound, such as in 'green' and 'funny'. However, in a Northern accent, this may not be the case, instead using the /ee/ sound for 'green' and the /e/ sound in 'funny'. This can also be seen in words like 'book' and 'could', which both use the short /oo/ in a Southern English accent. However, in some Northern accents the word 'book' may use the long /oo/ sound, while the word 'could' uses the short /oo/ sound.

Phase Five tricky words

Once children have started to learn about alternative pronunciations and spellings, previous tricky words they have learnt may become decodable for them. Words like 'me' and 'she' can be understood as using the grapheme 'e' that represents the /ee/ sound. Until now, learning tricky words by sight has been the only way for children to know how these common-exception words are pronounced. Phase Five still includes tricky words, which use some of the most uncommon spellings children will come across in their reading, as well as words with suffixes they will learn in Phase Six. It is therefore still important for children to learn these words by sight, rather than trying to sound them out, as this will benefit their fluency when reading.

List of Phase Five tricky words

oh
their
people
Mr
Mrs
looked
called
asked
would
should
could

Assessment

It is usually around this time that children will begin to prepare for, and then take, the phonics screening check. We will discuss this in the next chapter.

When reaching the end of Phase Five, children should be able to:

- say the corresponding sound for all graphemes learnt;
- apply phonics knowledge to read unfamiliar words and words that are not entirely decodable;
- read phonetically decodable two- and three-syllable words;
- write phonetically decodable two- and three-syllable words;
- read up to 100 high-frequency words;
- accurately spell most of the 100 high-frequency words;
- write each letter, formed correctly.

Introduction to Phase Six

There is some dispute about Phase Six and whether or not it should actually exist. In the DfE's *Letters and Sounds* (2007), Phase Six is the final phase of the systematic synthetic phonics programme. In some settings and in some phonics schemes, Phase Five is considered to be the final phase, with children continuing to become more fluent readers and accurate spellers without another phase to follow. Nevertheless, Phase Six is important to know about when teaching systematic synthetic phonics and the complexities of the English language.

By now, children will be able to read hundreds of words, including those using the most common grapheme–phoneme correspondences (GPCs). Children will still be developing their reading skills and using the new information they learnt in Phase Five to read unfamiliar words and words with more than one syllable. Children will read some words by sight, especially those that are very familiar to them and high-frequency words. They will also be using decoding, often very quickly and even silently as they have become so skilled at blending, or aloud if the word is a bit trickier.

At this stage children will also need to become more familiar with the rarer GPCs that we came across in Phase Five. These graphemes will appear more as children read a wider variety of texts, many of which will be longer and include more complex vocabulary. Children will also need to know when to use these rarer GPCs in their spelling. In Phase Six, the emphasis is on reading fluency and accurate spelling, while focusing on comprehension, past tense and adding suffixes to words.

Past tense

Learning how to write words using their past tense can at first appear fairly easy, simply adding a suffix such as '-ed' to words ('walk' becomes 'walked', etc.). However, many words have irregular past tenses, which complicates things a bit; 'go' becomes 'went', 'hold' becomes 'held', 'buy' becomes 'bought' and so on. Some words don't even change at all when in past tense, such as 'put' or 'cost'. It is important then to first teach children about the concept of past tense, and the spelling later on.

To introduce the concept of past tense, we can use the words 'today' and 'yesterday' to talk about activities. Perhaps you will read a diary entry from 'yesterday' which reads, 'Today I am swimming at the pool', and ask the children what you did yesterday. In their response, they should be using the past tense, for example, 'yesterday you *swam* in the pool'. This is known as 'simple past tense', but children may also respond with continuous past tense, such as 'yesterday you *were* swimming in the pool'. Oral activities like this can help children to understand what past tense is and when we use it. This is also an opportunity for practitioners to assess how much children understand about the past tense and identify any misconceptions, such as adding the suffix '-ed' when it is not needed: for example, 'goed' instead of 'went' or 'runned' instead of 'ran'.

Suffixes

When teaching children about suffixes, we usually begin with the suffix '-ed'. First, give the children present tense words which can be made into past tense by adding '-ed'. Give children phoneme frames to help them write the words with the suffix. This can help to reinforce the understanding of the sound 'ed' makes at the end of a word, as it does not always make the same sound. For example, 'ed' sounds different in 'jumped' and 'wanted'. Go through multiple words with the '-ed' suffix and show that even though the sound is different in some words, the spelling rule remains the same.

Other suffixes children will learn include '-ing', '-er', '-est', '-ful' '-ly', 'y' and plurals.

Activities for Phase Six

Activity: Present to past tense

Give children a piece of text written in present tense. It can be helpful to use the word 'today' to reinforce the tense. Ask the children to rewrite the passage using past tense. Remind the children that they can change 'today' to 'yesterday' and some other words will need to change to become past tense. You may wish to provide a table with examples of how to change certain words from present to past tense for children to reference.

Activity: Spelling pattern investigation

Give children a base word, such as 'hope'. Go through a list of suffixes you have learnt so far, seeing if they can be added to the base word. For example, we can make 'hopeful', 'hoping' and 'hoped', but cannot add the suffixes '-ly' or '-est'. You can write out the words in a table with the suffixes as headings. Discuss the spelling of each word and what has happened to the 'e' at the end of 'hope' when each suffix is added. Next, give the children a new base word and go through the suffixes again. After three or four words, ask the children if they notice any patterns in the spellings when suffixes are added. For example, when adding '-ful' the base word isn't changed, but when adding '-ing' the words ending in a vowel have it removed (hoping, joking, making).

Activity: Word builder

Provide the children with one bowl of base words and one bowl of suffixes. A child should take one card from each bowl and put them together. If they make a real word (such as 'joke' + '-ing'), the child will need to decide which spelling rule they need to use before writing the word down. If the base word and suffix do not make a real word together (such as 'help' and '-ly') then the cards can go back into the bowl and new cards should be drawn. You may wish to give the children a target number of words to create, such as a list of five or ten.

Activity: Rare GPC sentences

Discuss with the children some rare GPCs covered in Phase Five, such as 'ui' in 'bruise'. Ask the children if they can think of any other words that use the same grapheme for this phoneme. With these words written down, ask the children to work together to make a sentence using all of the words. There may be some funny creations here! An example may be, 'I ate some fruit in my favourite suit, then went on a cruise but bumped my head and got a bruise!'

Spelling rules

Below are some useful guidelines (or rules) for spelling. As a practitioner, it can be helpful to have these to hand when children ask why something is spelt a certain way (or why it isn't!). It can be helpful for children to know some of these rules so they can apply them when reading and writing.

/ai/ and /oi/

'ai' and 'oi' never appear at the end of words. Instead, we use the graphemes 'ay' and 'oy' for these sounds, such as in 'play' and 'joy'. This still applies if a suffix is added, like in 'played' or 'joyful'. When being used in a different position (other than the end of a word), the /ai/ sound is usually represented by 'ai' or 'a', such as in 'rain' or 'acorn'. The /oi/ sound is represented by 'oi' if it is not at the end of a word (or right before a suffix).

/o/ as 'a'

When the /o/ sound follows a 'w', it is usually spelt using an 'a', such as in 'water', 'wash' and 'was'. This also sometimes applies if the /w/ sound comes from the grapheme 'qu', such as in 'squash'.

/ur/ after 'w'

When the /ur/ sound follows the letter 'w', it is usually spelt using the 'or' grapheme, such as in 'word', 'worm' and 'work'. Of course, the common-exception word for this rule is 'were', which children will be familiar with as one of the tricky words learnt in Phase Four.

/or/ before /l/

When the /or/ sound comes before the /l/ phoneme, it is usually spelt with an 'a', such as in 'all', 'ball' and 'always'.

Words ending in /v/

Words do not usually end with the letter 'v'. Instead, words ending in the /v/ sound should be spelt with an 'e' on the end, such as in 'have' and 'give'. This can be a bit confusing, as this spelling rule makes it look as if a word contains a split digraph when it does not. There aren't many words that fit in this category though, so children often pick them up as a form of sight word earlier on.

When 'c' becomes /s/

The letter 'c' represents the /s/ sound when it comes before the letters 'e', 'i' or 'y', such as in the words 'cell', 'city' and 'cyan'.

'i' before 'e' except after 'c', but not really

You may remember being taught this spelling rule at school: 'i' before 'e' except after 'c'. However, this really doesn't work for the majority of words and often has 'but not always' tacked on the end! This rule only applies to words when the 'ie' or 'ei' is representing the /ee/ sound *and* follows a 'c', such as in 'receive' and 'ceiling'. There aren't many words that contain an /ee/ sound following the letter 'c', so it is better for children to simply learn the spelling of these words, rather than trying to apply the 'i before e except after c' rule as it usually ends up being unhelpful.

Contractions

The apostrophe in contractions goes in place of the missing letters. For example, 'could not' becomes 'couldn't', with the apostrophe marking where the 'o' would have been. We can see this in other contractions where more than one letter is omitted, such as in 'I'd' for 'I would' and 'you've' for 'you have'.

Comprehension

Children will have been developing their comprehension skills from the very beginning, starting in Phase One understanding words and their meanings, and later when listening to and reading stories to understand the narrative, make predictions and infer how characters might feel. Once they have reached Phase Six, children will be reading much longer, more complex texts. Their skills of inference and deduction will be necessary for them to go beyond literal meanings and understanding the deeper significance of particular passages. Children will use a range of strategies in their comprehension, such as summarising, using prior knowledge, clarifying meanings by using a dictionary or thesaurus (thus further building their vocabulary), questioning what they have read and creating mental images when reading (although not all children can do this, as not everyone generates images in their mind when thinking (Aphantasia Network, 2019)).

Misconceptions

At this stage, some children may still be struggling with identifying digraphs and trigraphs (or even quadgraphs, such as 'ough' in 'through') in words when reading. A child may continue to segment unfamiliar words by saying a sound for every letter, such as /r/ /a/ /i/ /n/ /c/ /o/ /a/ /t/ instead of /r/ /ai/ /n/ /c/ /oa/ /t/. This misconception should be identified as soon as possible and children should be supported to develop this skill. Sometimes practitioners must consider going back to an earlier phase of phonics and building up a child's skills from where they currently stand, rather than trying to teach more complicated phonics skills and plugging gaps along the way. A strong foundation is the only way for children to become confident, fluent and independent readers and spellers.

There will be a lot of misconceptions when it comes to spelling, due to the complex spelling rules of the English language and how often these are 'broken'. Providing resources for children to refer to for alternative GPCs and spelling rules can be helpful in supporting children to become more independent when reading and writing. Knowing some spelling rules, such as when adding suffixes or those listed above, can also help children to determine how to read or spell a word independently, as well as knowing how to spell high-frequency words automatically.

Assessment

We do not assess children at the end of Phase Six as there isn't really an 'end' of this phase. Children will continue to use the skills they have learnt to become fluent, confident readers and writers.

Conclusion

Phase Five and Phase Six are designed to create more independent, skilled and fluent readers. Introducing split digraphs, as well as alternative spellings and pronunciations, is a big task. It requires children to have a very solid understanding of phonics before getting to Phase Five, and being able to apply their new knowledge when both reading and writing. Children will continue to develop their spelling skills and understanding of spelling rules, which can be very complicated at times! As children are able to read more texts, their comprehension skills will also grow and they will be able to enjoy a wide variety of texts such as stories, poems, magazines, non-fiction books and more.

PART 2

In Part 2 we discuss the many other aspects of phonics to consider once a practitioner has a solid understanding of systematic synthetic phonics and its phases. The well-known phonics screening check is the assessment given to Year 1 children to assess their decoding skills. However, it does require preparation due to its unique approach, using both real words and pseudo-words to assess children. It is important that practitioners understand the check and how to support children before and during the assessment.

Practitioners must also consider the provision and environment they provide for children, to immerse them in a phonics-rich space to further support their learning. This includes knowing the most effective ways to support children with special educational needs and disabilities, to make phonics accessible and inclusive for all children.

5
Phonics Screening Check

This chapter will cover:

1. the purpose of the phonics screening check;
2. how to prepare children for the check;
3. pseudo-words or 'alien words';
4. activities to support decoding skills;
5. who should not take the check;
6. how to deliver the check;
7. what happens after the check;
8. criticism of the check.

Introduction

The phonics screening check is an assessment designed to identify if a child has learnt the decoding skills they need to be able to read. To do this, the check uses both real words and 'psuedo-words', also known as 'alien words', 'nonsense words' or 'silly words'. The idea behind pseudo-words (words made up of letters that don't create a real English word) is that if a child has the relevant decoding skills, they will be able to segment and blend to read the word whether it makes sense or not. Next to each pseudo-word in the check is an image of an alien, to let the child know it is not a real word, but an alien word.

The check happens in June for children who will have reached age six by the end of that academic year; for children in schools, this means the check is carried out in Year 1. Some children will take the check in Year 2, either as a retake having not passed the year before, or for the first time if they did not take the check in Year 1. The check is statutory, starting in 2012 after being piloted by 300 schools in 2011. There are some exceptions that can be made for children on an individual basis, such as a child with particular special educational needs or disabilities (SEND) that the check would not be accessible for.

The check is taken in a 1:1 setting. The words children need to read are in a booklet which the children go through with the practitioner. The practitioner giving the check is not allowed to give the child any feedback during the assessment, but can encourage them to continue. We will look further into the rules of the check later in this chapter.

Structure

The check is made up of two parts: Section 1 and Section 2. The words become more complex as children go through the check, with 40 words in total to read.

Section 1

Section 1 includes:

- a range of simple word structures and letter combinations;
- VC, VCC, CVC, CVCC and CCVC words;
- single letter sounds (a, b, c, d, e, f, g, h, i, j, k, l, m, n, o, p, q(u), u, r, s, t, u, v, w, x, y, z);
- consonant digraphs such as ff, ss, zz, ll and ck, sh, ch and th;
- high-frequency vowel digraphs such as ee, oi, or and ar (the sounds for each will remain consistent).

The structure of Section 1 is as follows:

- page 1: four pseudo-words;
- page 2: four pseudo-words;
- page 3: four pseudo-words;

- page 4: four real words;
- page 5: four real words.

Section 1 examples

Past checks can be found on the DfE's website. You can also find practise videos on the Little Learners Education YouTube channel, @LittleLearnersVideos.

Section 1
Page 1:
(Each word would have an alien picture next to it)
ot
ult
zik
luf

Page 2:
(Each word would have an alien picture next to it)
barg
lorsh
jeng
chuv

Page 3:
(Each word would have an alien picture next to it)
pleeb
kran
jopt
reets

Page 4:
at
fill

mark

crack

Page 5:

rust

shop

swim

coins

Section 2

Section 2 includes:

- a range of more complex word structures and letter combinations;
- CCVCC, CCCVC, CCCVCC (and so on) and two-syllable words;
- GPCs from Section 1 as well as the following:
    - other consonant digraphs such as 'ph' and 'wh'
    - lower-frequency vowel digraphs such as 'ai', 'au', 'aw', 'ay', 'ea', 'er', 'ew', 'ir', 'oa', 'ou', 'ow', 'oy', 'ue' and 'ur'
    - split digraphs (a-e, e-e, i-e, o-e, u-e)
    - trigraphs, such as 'air' and 'igh'
    - alternative pronunciations, such as for 'a' (acorn), 'c' (city), 'ch' (chef), 'e' (evil), 'ea' (bread), 'er' (baker), 'g' (germ), 'i' (find), 'ie' (field), 'o' (no), 'ou' (should), 'ow' (own), 's' (is), 'u' (music), 'ue' (blue) and 'u-e' (tube).

The structure of Section 2 is as follows:

- page 6: four pseudo-words;
- page 7: four pseudo-words;
- page 8: four real words;
- page 9: four real words;
- page 10: four real words.

The check usually takes less than ten minutes to complete, but there is no time limit.

Section 2 examples

Past checks can be found on the DfE website. You can also find practise videos on the Little Learners Education YouTube channel, @LittleLearnersVideos.

Section 2

Page 6:

(Each word would have an alien picture next to it)

whive

ter

shurl

yawm

Page 7:

(Each word would have an alien picture next to it)

plake

fraind

glept

troont

Page 8:

germ

boy

goat

book

Page 9:

dreamt

stripe

whale

cloud

Page 10:
uniform
owner
whirling
fabrics

Preparing for the check

During the year leading up to the phonics screening check, practitioners will work on preparing children by supporting them to learn the skills they need to decode a range of words. Alongside this, practitioners will introduce the concept of alien words, nonsense words that don't make sense in our language, but may do in an alien language! It is important to emphasise that alien words are not real words, so will (and should) sound silly. Without knowing this, many children will read an alien word and, although they have segmented and blended correctly, try to think of what real word it *could* be. For example, if a child reads the alien word 'skept', they may try to make sense of it and instead give the answer of 'slept' because that is a real word.

It is vital throughout the year to identify any gaps in a child's phonics knowledge in order to put support in place and correct misconceptions. As well as targeted interventions, it is helpful to offer a range of reading materials for children that follow their interests. Although child-led learning is more prevalent in Early Years, it is still beneficial in later year groups to create engaging activities for children that are more focused on their individual needs and interests.

Activity ideas to prepare for the phonics screening check

Below are some activities you can use with children to both prepare them for the phonics screening check and consolidate their decoding skills.

Activity: Dog and Quog

Decorate two boxes: one as a dog face and one as an alien face. Ensure each box has an opening for the 'mouth'. The dog is referred to as 'Dog' and the alien as 'Quog'.

Provide cards with real words and alien words on them, ensuring they are small enough to fit through the 'mouths' of Dog and Quog. The words on the cards can be adjusted to meet the children's current level of understanding and decoding skills. You may wish to use the parameters set out in Section 1 and Section 2 of the check (discussed earlier) to create the word cards. Children will need to decode each word and decide if it is a real word or an alien word. If it is a real word, it should be 'fed' to Dog. If it is an alien word, it should be fed to Quog. Once children are familiar with this activity, you may wish to encourage them to write their own cards, creating both real words and their own made-up alien words.

Activity: Stepping stones

This game can be played as a smaller version at a table, or as a large version in the outdoor area. For the table version, create a 'river' using blue material, paper or card. Next, place 'stepping stones' across the river in two columns. Alternate which stepping stones have a real word written on them and which have pseudo-words written on them (do not have one category of words all in the same column). Children can use a small figure, like a counting bear or Lego person and help them get across the river. To do so, their figure can only stand on real words. Children need to read each word to decide which stepping stone their figure should step on. For the larger, outdoor version of this game, create a giant river with chalk and set out large stepping stones across it with the real and pseudo-words written on them. Instead of using a toy figure, children take themselves across the river, finding the real words along the way to safely get to the other side.

Activity: Astronaut words

Put up real and alien words around the room. You may even wish to decorate the room to make it look like space, with stars, planets and blacked-out windows. Children should dress up like astronauts and pretend they are on a special space mission, trying to learn more about aliens. To do this, they must find alien words and bring them back to Earth. Children should walk around the space and decode the words they find. If they find an alien word, it should be put into their bag, ready to be taken back to Earth. Along the way, children will also need to decode real words but leave them where they are. At the end of the activity, 'back on Earth', go through the words in the bag, decoding each word together. Did any real words end up inside? Were any alien words missed? What could each of these words mean in the alien language?

Activity: Alien word bingo

Create bingo cards that contain only alien words. Ensure the complexity of the words is suitable for the child or children using the cards (refer again to Section 1 and Section 2 of the check when planning). Children can use counters or a pen to cover the words they have that match the words you call out. Just like in normal bingo, the child who covers a full row of words can shout, 'Bingo!' and wins the game.

Activity: Name that alien

Give the children some pictures of aliens and ask them to think of a name for each of them. The names cannot be real words – they must be nonsense words. Once the children have chosen a name, ask them to spell it. They can work together or individually to decide how the word should be spelt, using their knowledge of GPCs. Children can also compare their spellings and discuss how sometimes a word spelt in a different way can sound the same (for example, 'spleeb' and 'spleab').

Activity: @LittleLearnersVideos YouTube video

On the Little Learners Education YouTube channel, we have a video for children to practise sounding out alien words called *Alien Words: Phonics Screening Check* (available at: www.youtube.com/watch?v=N8wsIajrsZE&ab_channel=LittleLearners). The video shows how to decode a variety of pseudo-words, using sound buttons as a visual aid.

Activity: Past papers

The phonics screening check materials from past years can be found on the DfE's website (Standards and Testing Agency, 2025a). This shows exactly what the check will look like, including the layout and the alien pictures children might see when they take the check themselves. It can be really helpful to show children past papers to familiarise them with what the materials look like. You don't have to tell the children that these are past papers, or even that the phonics screening check exists. By using past papers, either on the board or with hard copies, this can help children feel less anxious or overwhelmed when presented with the actual check under more formal conditions.

Who should not take the check?

Ultimately, headteachers have the final say on who should not take the phonics screening check. Parents should always be notified about this. There are a range of reasons as to why a child may not take the check, which can include:

- working below the expected level of development;
- very little knowledge of GPCs;
- English as an additional language, depending on fluency and understanding (for example, a child who has just started learning English may struggle with the check);
- non-verbalism;
- selective mutism: these children may take the check at home, in a comfortable setting and with an adult they can speak freely around. The adult can then discuss the outcome with the teacher. This will not count as an official taking of the check but allows the child to show what they know and share the skills they have learnt. This arrangement can only take place after the check's official period ends, to ensure security of the check materials;
- using British Sign Language (BSL) or other sign-supported communication to spell out words. For these children, the check is not accessible, and the assessment of their reading skills must be undertaken in a more appropriate way.

This is not an exhaustive list and there may be other reasons a headteacher decides that a child should not take the check. A child who does not take the check may be eligible to take it the following year, depending on the individual circumstances.

During the check

The phonics screening check is carried out in a 1:1 setting. This is a statutory test and so while the setting shouldn't feel too formal to the child in order to put them at ease, practitioners must be mindful of the rules of giving the check.

Make sure the environment is appropriate: not too noisy and well lit, and that any displays that may help children complete the check have been covered. If more than one practitioner is carrying out the check, ensure that children are in separate spaces, so they are not distracted or helped by each other reading the words.

Consider any access needs, which may include:

- *rest breaks*: children can take a rest break between each section of the test, or more frequently if they need to. The check can be modified to include fewer words on each page. During rest breaks, children should be monitored and must not have any contact with children who have already taken the check. The check must be completed on the same day it is started;
- *cued speech*: children with hearing impairment who used cued speech may use this during the check. Cued speech involves a variety of hand shapes to make spoken language more visible and easier to understand when it comes to mouth shapes that are the same for a number of sounds (for example, /m/, /b/ and /p/). Cued speech can be used by someone who is trained to use it, either to understand what sound the child is using, or if the child prefers to only verbally say the words, the practitioner can use cued speech to confirm the sounds the child has used;
- *visual phonics*: children who usually use visual phonics can do so during the check. Visual phonics is a group of hand gestures that each represent a different phoneme (unlike other sign-supported communications in which hand gestures represent graphemes);
- *sound buttons*: children can mark sound buttons under each word if they usually do this to read. Practitioners must provide a clean copy of the check for the child to do this and must not mark any sound buttons for the child;
- *braille*: the check is available in braille and should be provided for children who need it;
- *adapted materials*: practitioners can download the check materials in advance and adapt them to meet the needs of children, such as changing the font type or size, colours, number of words on each page, etc.;
- *alternative location*: at the headteacher's discretion, the check can take place in a different location. Rules for this can be found on the DfE's website (Standards and Testing Agency, 2025b).

Readers are not allowed for the check and cannot be used as an adaptation for access needs in this case.

The check has no time limit, but usually children complete it in ten minutes or less. The practitioner and child will sit with the check booklet in front of them, going through each word on each page. Practitioners will mark on their answer sheet whether the child was correct or incorrect when reading each word.

Before starting the check, explain what is going to happen. For example: 'Today we are going to read some words. Some are real words and some are alien words. The alien words will have funny alien pictures next to them! You can sound the words out if you're not sure what they say, and you can correct yourself if you make a mistake. Making mistakes is absolutely fine – it's how we learn! If you find a word too tricky to read, don't worry, we can just move onto the next one. Let's have some fun reading these words!'

Practitioners usually have a good idea of how a child will perform during the check, having been regularly assessing them formatively throughout the year. However, there are many variables that can have an impact: did the child eat enough breakfast? Did they fall over on the way to school? Did they sleep well last night? It is important to keep this in mind and allow children the time they need to complete the check.

Practitioners can point at each word to show the child which word to read next, but must not point at words in a way that shows how the word should be decoded. You can offer encouragement, but cannot indicate to the child whether they have read the word correctly or incorrectly. Practitioners can give children as long as they need to read a word and can decide if it is appropriate to move onto the next word instead.

After the check

Once the check has been carried out schools must report to their local authority. Practitioners must also inform parents/carers about whether or not their child passed the check. Practitioners should analyse children's results and put support in place for those children who scored too low to pass the check. Not passing the check suggests that a child does not have the decoding skills expected at this stage and therefore needs further support to develop these skills, whether that is by learning GPCs, working on segmenting and blending or revising alternative pronunciations. Practitioners have a responsibility to identify which children need additional support and to put relevant plans in place to support them. Any children who do not pass the check the first time will take the check again the following academic year: this is the year they turn seven, which is usually Year 2 in schools.

The DfE does not publish school-level results of the phonics screening check, but there will be local authority, regional and national results for practitioners to view and use to benchmark children's results against.

Criticism

Like most things in education, the phonics screening check does not come without criticism. The fact children are being assessed formally at all is often a topic of debate. With the check, though, there are some more specific concerns. For example, pseudo-words can be confusing for children who are confident readers as they may decode the word correctly, but then try to think of a real word that is the closest fit. This is one reason it is so important to prepare children for the concept of alien words. Not being able to give children feedback during the check can also be difficult for many children who are used to being given feedback in real time, which is the practice of many practitioners and in many classrooms. Some children who are more anxious may take the absence of feedback as a sign that they have decoded the word incorrectly, even if they haven't. Children who struggle with segmenting, blending, GPCs and those children who struggle to identify digraphs and trigraphs – instead reading them as individual graphemes – will also struggle with the check. In some cases, these children may be exempt from taking the check based on the exclusionary criteria we discussed earlier.

One study conducted by the Education Policy Institute (EPI) looked at a range of factors since the introduction of the phonics screening check. It found that not only was there no evidence that the introduction of the check had any positive impact on reading results in Key Stage 1 or Key Stage 2, but there was also no evidence it had improved the attainment gaps by the end of primary school (Campbell and Kelly, 2024). Of course, the purpose of the check is not to necessarily improve outcomes, but to assess whether or not children have obtained the expected decoding skills for their age and stage. However, this does raise the question of if the check is for the benefit of children or not; if not, should we be doing it? Perhaps teacher assessment could be a better fit to ascertain the level of decoding children are working at. From the teachers who responded to the study, over half of Key Stage 1 teachers think the check should be scrapped (Campbell and Kelly, 2024).

The EPI also found that there is 'a relationship between not passing the [phonics screening check] and being identified as having special educational needs and/or disabilities (SEND)', with these children being more likely to be recorded as having SEND in Year 2 (Campbell and Kelly, 2024). This could be interpreted as a positive thing, with children needing additional support being identified. However, it could also indicate that children are being labelled as having SEND simply because they did not meet the standard to pass the check, even though they do not have any SEND.

Conclusion

Whatever your view, the phonics screening check seems to be here to stay for now. Children often find the concept of alien words very entertaining and a fun challenge. It is up to practitioners to make this learning as engaging and positive as possible, while noticing any misconceptions and putting interventions in place to support the children in their care. Understanding the purpose of the check and how to prepare children for it is an important part of a Key Stage 1 teacher's role (particularly those in Year 1), as is knowing how best to support children through the check in a way that is most relevant to them.

6
Phonics in Provision

This chapter will cover:

1. what 'provision' means;
2. continuous provision in the EYFS;
3. continuous provision in KS1;
4. enabling environments;
5. how phonics provision relates to the *Teachers' Standards*.

Introduction

The term 'provision' refers to the environment, resources, activities and opportunities children have access to in their school or setting. For phonics, there are so many aspects of classroom provision that can lend themselves to effective and engaging learning opportunities, as well as encouraging independence and confidence when reading and writing.

As you will have seen, there are many activities in this book that can support children in their phonics learning, from Phase One all the way through to Phase Six. We can also consider wider provision to immerse children in phonics learning, even when not taking part in more structured and planned activities. This can look different from setting to setting and when comparing the Early Years Foundation Stage to Key Stage 1.

Continuous provision in EYFS

In the Early Years Foundation Stage (EYFS), *continuous provision* refers to all of the resources, learning spaces and activities that children have access to at all times. Continuous provision encourages independence, exploration and learning through child-led play. There are so many opportunities to include phonics in continuous provision, some of which have already been outlined in this book.

In an Early Years setting, the focus is on child-led learning through play. This lends itself very easily to the concept of continuous provision, as children can 'free-flow' between different areas, activities and even environments. Children should be able to access indoor and outdoor spaces and engage in a range of resources and activities which cover multiple areas of development in the EYFS.

While children in Reception may be introduced to new graphemes and phonemes in a more formal way (sat on a carpet, listening and attending for an extended period of time), the way they engage with phonics at all other times should encourage independence and exploration. Phonics can be incorporated into many areas of the setting, such as:

- opportunities for developing communication and language skills when collaborating with peers, such as with small-world play, role play, group games and areas for exploration including outdoor environments;
- grapheme cards: for example, 'f' in the water tray with toy fish, or 'sh' in the role play area which is set up as a shop;
- phonics zone: an interactive display table that changes weekly (or more frequently if appropriate), with objects starting with sounds learnt, CVC words to read, tactile letters, sand to mark-make in, etc.;
- access to mark-making resources both inside and outside, such as pencils, paper, chalk, paintbrushes, paint, water, etc.;
- opportunities for writing: graphemes to copy, pictures for prompts, tracing, plain and lined paper and whiteboards;
- messy play: for example, coloured rice to sieve through to find letters or words, or shaving foam to write letters in with fingers or brushes;
- loose parts and natural resources like sticks, leaves and conkers to use to make the shape of graphemes learnt;
- lots of opportunities for talking and using the sounds learnt, either through planned activities or planning in the moment based on children's interests and own ideas;

- displays around the environment to support grapheme–phoneme correspondence, decoding and writing; this could include graphemes learnt, pictures with CVC words or even an I-spy board (a display covered in different objects which encourages children to identify initial sounds in words when playing the game);
- access to resources like phonics puzzles, voice buttons (to record the adult or child's voice), magnetic letters and noise makers or instruments.

Continuous provision in Key Stage 1

Traditionally, continuous provision ends with the Early Years. However, many settings and practitioners have realised the benefit of using continuous provision in Year 1 and even beyond. We know that the years from birth to age five are extremely significant, with 90 per cent of brain growth happening during this period of time (NHS, n.d.). However, many pedagogical theorists and practitioners consider the period between ages two and seven to be the 'prime opportunity to lay the foundation for a holistic education for children' (Sriram, 2020), due to this being a critical phase of brain development. Why then, do we stop giving children access to opportunities for independent learning and exploration? For many settings, the EYFS way of learning is seen as just preparation for 'real' school and learning, which is certainly not the correct way to view this stage of education! Many practitioners in Key Stage 1 are concerned about the demands of the national curriculum, which is understandable, but there are ways to incorporate continuous provision and child-led learning even when moving from the EYFS framework to the national curriculum.

Some Key Stage 1 settings will incorporate elements of continuous provision in the autumn term for a smoother transition from Reception to Year 1, slowly phasing this out as the year progresses. Some will use continuous provision all year, while other settings do not use continuous provision at all once children enter Year 1.

Knowing the benefits continuous provision can have when it comes to phonics learning (and indeed other forms of learning), means incorporating this style of provision could help improve outcomes and lead to more engagement from children. Of course, this would mean developing a space and planning that both builds on the EYFS framework and focuses on the requirements of the national curriculum. Whether a Key Stage 1 class is using continuous provision or not, it is always important to consider the environment children will be learning in, which is what we will discuss next.

Enabling environments

The environment children learn in is an integral part of the learning process. For many, the main environment will be their classroom, but this can also be other common areas in a school or setting, outside or even at another location. Enabling environments allow children to thrive by offering them a safe, inclusive, comfortable and secure space to engage in a wide range of experiences and opportunities. We know children learn best through play, particularly in the Early Years, so enabling environments should offer opportunities to move around, be active, collaborate with others and use their imagination. Providing open-ended resources and activities in provision can 'enable children to access and combine processes of development and learning' (EYC, 2021).

Creating such an environment can seem much easier through continuous provision in Early Years settings, but what can an enabling environment look like in Key Stage 1 and beyond? Some Key Stage 1 classrooms incorporate elements of continuous provision, but not all do. However, it is still possible to create a comfortable, inclusive and engaging environment which supports children's independence and creativity.

Typically, phonics teaching in Year 1 involves daily lessons to revise previous sounds learnt, introducing a new sound or alternative spelling, reading with this new phoneme or grapheme and an opportunity to write it, often using individual whiteboards. Children are also introduced to new tricky words and will be exposed to these words more in their reading and writing. Children will then use their new and prior phonics knowledge to read a range of texts and write with increasing independence and accuracy. In classrooms without continuous provision, adult-led activities are the focus and often follow topics or themes throughout the year. Phonics skills and development are incorporated into these activities or tasks, with differentiation either by outcome or by scaffolding and support.

Below are some more ideas for including phonics provision in the environment, even if continuous provision is not used.

Working displays

These are displays which can be created, added to and modified over time with the children, depending on what they have learnt. For example, in the first term of Reception, children may add a new grapheme to the display board each day, as well as pictures of items that start with each sound. This may then change to children adding CVC words they have been decoding or even writing. As children move through their learning, the working display (sometimes known as a *working wall*) evolves, showing the progress children have made and giving them an area to reflect on their learning.

Pre-prepared displays

These boards can also be helpful, giving children a place to find guidance for particular aspects of phonics. The graphemes can be displayed with a picture clue beside them, allowing children to find the one they need and be reminded of its phoneme, or copy the letter formation when writing.

Sound and word banks

These are usually an A5 or A4 piece of paper with information children need to help them complete their tasks, whether that is reading, writing or completing other phonics activities. These can help with differentiation and independence. Sound banks can have graphemes on them with pictures of objects that start with that sound, which helps children to locate the grapheme they need and recall the sound it makes. This can help children feel more independent and confident when reading. Sound banks for children working in later phonics phases may include alternative spellings for particular phonemes and words or pictures that reflect that sound, helping children to remember the many pronunciations certain graphemes may have. Word banks may include tricky words, words with alternative spellings or other words children are working on to help them in their writing, allowing children to find the spelling they need without disrupting the flow of their writing.

Book corner

Even in later year groups, classrooms and other settings should include a book corner. This provides a selection of books and a comfortable place to read. Perhaps children are able to choose a book to read if they finish work early or even have allocated reading time during the day or week. The book corner should be stocked with books that are not only appropriate for the children's reading level, but also follow some of their interests. There should be a mix of fiction and non-fiction books to read. Promoting reading for pleasure is important and some practitioners even plan reading time into their day, with the whole class, including the adults, reading independently for a certain amount of time.

Books for all topics

Whether it's small-world play (playing with small toys and figures to act out a narrative – for example, farm animals and a barn) in a nursery room or a science lesson in a Year 2 classroom, books can play a role. In the EYFS, books that are related to the activities in provision can be placed next to them, giving children the option of looking at a book as well as accessing the activity. For example, in a role-play corner made to look like a rocket ship, you may find a non-fiction book about space and a fiction book about aliens. In later year groups, there may be a small table or shelf dedicated to books related to the topics being taught that week that children can have access to at any time. These books can be swapped for others when the topic changes or a particular event or celebration is taking place.

Instruments

For very young children working at Phase One or Phase Two, instruments are often accessible, and children can freely explore the different sounds they make. As children get older, instruments are often locked away, saved only for music lessons. However, having a range of instruments that children can access can be beneficial at any stage. For example, perhaps a child in Year 1 is writing a story and needs to describe the sound of a storm. Using shakers or a drum could help them to think of words that describe those sounds, which they can then include in their writing.

Teachers' Standards

The *Teachers' Standards* (DfE, 2021), set out by the DfE, state the minimum requirements for a teacher's practice once they have qualified teacher status (QTS). The standards are used to assess trainee teachers and also fully qualified teachers, whether that be for an appraisal or some form of observation. When it comes to the *Teachers' Standards*, effective phonics provision falls under six of them (there are eight in total).

1. *Set high expectations which inspire, motivate and challenge pupils*
   Creating an environment rich with phonics resources and activities inspires children to interact with letters and sounds in their play and when engaging with the world around them. We can motivate children by giving them access to both the tools they need and resources that can encourage them to try tasks they may not have been confident to attempt before. By having high expectations of all children, we can encourage them to progress through a systematic synthetic phonics (SSP) programme and gain confidence while doing so by being appropriately challenged.
2. *Promote good progress and outcomes by pupils*
   Offering an enabling environment with continuous access to phonics resources to support learning allows children to progress. Practitioners can observe children's interaction with phonics provision to assess what they can do independently and what they may need to progress to the next stage of their learning. This allows practitioners to plan next steps and target support.
3. *Demonstrate good subject and curriculum knowledge*
   Reading this book will certainly help you with this one! By now, you will have a good understanding of how phonics plays a pivotal role in children's education. It begins with their early listening and speaking skills and grows into the ability to effectively communicate, read and write. You will demonstrate this knowledge through the way you teach and the provision you provide, including being able to differentiate for individual needs and be able to identify when children may have gaps in their phonics knowledge. You will be able to use your knowledge of the phonics phases, segmenting and blending, GPCs and the way SSP works to correct misconceptions and offer appropriate support.
4. *Plan and teach well-structured lessons*
   Knowing as much about phonics as you now do, you will be able to plan well-structured lessons that involve appropriate differentiation and teach with confidence, able to notice misconceptions quickly and identify when children need more support. You can plan lessons using your understanding of SSP to teach using a structured approach.
5. *Adapt teaching to respond to the strengths and needs of all pupils*
   Knowing about phonics from Phase One to Phase Six, not just the phase the children in your care are working on, allows you as a practitioner to notice gaps in learning and be able to respond quickly to the needs of all children. If a child is struggling with blending, you may decide to use some Phase One activities to help with this skill, because you know that without a secure foundation, children

will find new skills very difficult. Similarly, if a child is reading CVC words fluently and easily, you may decide to challenge them with some CCVC or CVCC words. The provision and planning in your setting will allow for children to work at their own pace, stage and at an appropriate level for their individual needs.

6. *Make accurate and productive use of assessment*

    Giving children more independence and opportunities for exploration allows practitioners to observe children's progress and continually be assessing. Practitioners can then use these assessments to plan for future provision and lesson content. In Reception, practitioners will use these skills to assess children's phonics against the early learning goals. Practitioners will continue to formatively assess children in Year 1 and use the summative assessment of the phonics screening check – which you are now very familiar with – to assess decoding skills.

Conclusion

No matter how your setting's provision is set up, there are a multitude of ways to incorporate phonics into your learning environment and to give children the opportunity for exploration, independence and child-led learning. Continuous provision in both the EYFS and KS1 has been shown to support children's development and promote good outcomes, but even settings without continuous provision can consider the provision they do offer and how they can inspire children by immersing them in the world of phonics. Using enabling environments to encourage children to develop new skills and become independent learners is an efficient and effective way to do this.

7
Supporting Phonics Learning for Children with Special Educational Needs and Disabilities

This chapter will cover:

1. how SSP can help support children with SEND when learning phonics and how to read;
2. supporting children with types of neurodiversity when teaching phonics, with a focus on autistic children, children with dyslexia and attention deficit (hyperactivity) disorder;
3. supporting children with hearing loss or deafness when teaching phonics;
4. criticisms of SSP as a method of teaching children with SEND.

Introduction

A huge part of an educational practitioner's role is to make sure that learning is inclusive and accessible for all children. For children with special educational needs and disabilities (SEND), this means that specific and individualised planning, differentiation and support must be considered. For children in the EYFS, play-based continuous provision and assessment through observation offers an ideal environment for children to work at their own pace and develop skills in their own time. Of course, there are countless different needs children could have – some which may be part of a diagnosed condition, others which are not. It is imperative that practitioners are able to identify possible additional needs to make sure children receive the learning approach best suited to them.

In this chapter, we will discuss types of neurodiversity such as autism, dyslexia and attention deficit hyperactivity disorder (ADHD), as well as disabilities such as hearing impairment and deafness. It is important to remember that each of these conditions is different for each child, and there are many other diagnoses and needs that can affect phonics learning other than those we will be discussing here. If you have a child in your care with specific needs, it can be helpful to seek out some professional development training to ensure you know as much as you can in order to support them. You should also work closely with your special educational needs and disabilities coordinator (SENDCo) to plan and review any support a child may need.

Autism

Autism exists on a spectrum. This means each autistic child will have a very individualised experience in terms of how they are affected. If a child is autistic this means their brain works differently to a *neurotypical* brain. Some autistic children will require little or no support, while others may need much more, including support from a carer. Autism can cause difficulties with processing information, so when learning phonics, instructions can be misunderstood, or it may take longer for an autistic child to process and remember the information they are learning. Knowing a child well and understanding their individual needs allows practitioners to differentiate effectively. There has been some debate about whether systematic synthetic phonics (SSP) is the best way to teach phonics to autistic children, but many studies have found that 'phonemic awareness, phonics, vocabulary, reading fluency, and reading comprehension ... is not only appropriate for children with autism but also effective' (Arciuli and Bailey, 2021, p. 226).

Knowing a child's strengths is just as important as understanding any challenges they may face. For many autistic children strengths may include attention to detail, a wealth of knowledge about their favourite topics, good memory, honesty and a strong sense of justice (Autistica, n.d.).

Approaches that can be helpful for autistic children learning phonics include:

- ensuring the child can learn in a calm and distraction-free environment;
- using rest breaks;
- keeping instructions simple, direct and with minimal steps;
- focusing on one sound at a time, ensuring understanding before moving on;
- not overwhelming the child with too many letter sounds at once;
- using visual cues such as pictures and flashcards;
- understanding the child's strengths and interests in order to plan appropriate opportunities for both child-led and adult-led activities that will appeal to that child;
- contextualising phonics by using words that are familiar and meaningful to them when segmenting and blending;
- incorporating phonics into play and other areas of learning to make it hands-on and as engaging as possible;
- using tangible resources, such as tactile letters, messy play and activities that involve moving objects around;
- incorporating movement into the learning. This could be using actions for sounds (such as in the *Jolly Phonics* scheme (Jolly Learning, 1987)) or moving around the environment rather than staying sat in one place;
- planning phonics activities and provision that relate to the child's interests;
- using technology to support understanding – some autistic children may prefer using a tablet to play phonics games or find voice recording buttons helpful for recall.

Dyslexia

Dyslexia is yet another way in which a brain can work differently to a neurotypical brain. About 10 per cent of the population have dyslexia, which can have an impact on phonological processing, reading and writing skills, as well as making processing information, remembering what is seen or heard and organisational skills difficult (BDA, n.d.). Children with dyslexia can also find listening and attending for long periods of time tricky and feel tired quickly when trying to concentrate for an extended period of time. Like all learning difficulties or additional needs, children with dyslexia will require different levels of support. Many children with dyslexia can suffer from frustration and low self-confidence if they do not receive appropriate support.

Many children with dyslexia display strengths such as being observant, having very good problem-solving skills, creativity and high levels of empathy. It is important to recognise the strengths of the child you are working with to plan learning that suits them best.

Approaches that can be helpful when teaching phonics to children with dyslexia include:

- keeping learning structured and revisiting prior learning often;
- focusing on hearing sounds and oral blending and segmenting first, being sure to revisit those Phase One skills even if the child is working on later phases;
- not being afraid to go back and revisit prior learning that a child seems to have forgotten, in order to rebuild that foundation again. Remember: learning is not always linear!
- using sound buttons under words to give children a visual clue about how to break up a word;
- encouraging the child to place their finger on each grapheme to help them read the sounds in the correct order;
- including rest breaks. Children with dyslexia can feel tired or even exhausted when concentrating for a period of time, so when working on phonics or reading together it is important to include rest breaks or to use a variety of short activities rather than one long ongoing task;
- using paired reading. Instead of the child reading independently, read together. This could be taking turns reading a sentence or page, saying a word the child is finding difficult, or decoding words together. This can help keep the flow of reading more fluent and raise self-confidence, as well as giving the child small breaks and a chance to see reading being modelled to them;
- using sans-serif fonts, larger text and particular-coloured backgrounds can be helpful for children with dyslexia. Using a light background (but not a white one) with dark text is best. It can also be helpful to break text up into shorter paragraphs or sentences, so children are not overwhelmed by the number of words on the page;
- covering text with a piece of paper and revealing one word or sentence at a time, to avoid distraction or confusion when seeing too many words on the page;
- using different technology to see what may support the child best. Some children respond well to phonics games on a computer or tablet or use an e-reader to read for pleasure, allowing them to still engage in listening to stories and learning information from non-fiction books.

Attention deficit hyperactivity disorder

Like the other neurodiversities we have discussed, ADHD means that the brain works differently to neurotypical brains. Children with ADHD can find it difficult to concentrate and can be easily distracted. They can find it hard to listen to and follow instructions and may be forgetful. However, children with ADHD can often be very creative, energetic and can notice small details.

Children with ADHD may seem fidgety; tapping, flapping or becoming restless and moving around when they are supposed to be sat down. They may also find it difficult to wait their turn, either in activities or in conversations. This difficulty with concentration and focus can make learning phonics tricky, as segmenting and blending can feel slow and repetitive.

For children with ADHD, their strengths may include periods of hyperfocus (when they are completely focused on one task), inventive and out-of-the-box thinking, creativity, resilience and willingness to try new things (Nordby et al., 2023).

Approaches that can be helpful when teaching phonics to children with dyslexia include:

- ensuring the learning environment is calm and free of distraction;
- rest breaks and movement breaks;
- making phonics as engaging and fun as possible;
- using audiobooks and e-readers when reading for pleasure, so children can still access and enjoy stories and learning information;
- using movement during tasks;
- highlighting tricky words or sounds the child finds difficult before reading, so the flow of their reading can be less interrupted;
- using visual cues;
- focusing on one skill or task at a time;
- utilising technology such as phonics apps and interactive resources.

Hearing loss and deafness

Phonics relies a lot on listening skills, which of course is a problem if a child cannot hear well, or at all. Eighty per cent of children will experience temporary deafness in one or both ears due to a condition called 'glue ear' by the time they are ten years old (NDCS, 2025). Many Early Years practitioners will be familiar with this condition as it is so common. Therefore, knowing how to support children with hearing loss is an important skill for all practitioners.

For children with permanent hearing loss or deafness, this may be mild, moderate or profound. In the UK there are more than 50,000 deaf children, 78 per cent of whom are educated in mainstream schools (NDCS, 2021). Some children may use technology such as hearing aids or cochlear implants to help them hear, but it is important to understand the limitations of these and that children may not want to use them at all times.

For practitioners working with children with hearing loss and deafness it is important to:

- have a clear understanding of the child's needs: is their hearing loss temporary, permanent, mild, moderate or profound?
- know how the child usually communicates at home: do they use spoken English, British Sign Language (BSL), Sign Supported English (SSE), cued speech or a combination of these?
- have a good understanding of what the child can hear and if this fluctuates;
- know if the child uses any technology, such as hearing aids or a cochlear implant, as well as how often they use them and what they can hear when not using them;
- understand what approach to take if a child's technology stops working;
- understand that hearing loss does not mean children are unable to develop a good understanding of phonics and spoken language.

Approaches to support children with hearing loss or deafness when learning phonics include:

- asking the child what methods they find most helpful when learning to read;
- using BSL or SSE;
- using visual phonics, which involves a group of hand gestures that each represent a different phoneme (unlike other sign-supported communications in which hand gestures represent graphemes);
- using cued speech, which involves hand movements by the mouth to signify a particular sound, particularly for sounds which look the same when spoken (for example /b/, /p/ and /m/);
- for hearing loss in one ear, ensuring practitioners sit on the correct side of the child when communicating with spoken English;
- using pictures cues to support phoneme and grapheme learning;

- setting high expectations: hearing loss does not mean children are unable to develop a good understanding of phonics and spoken language;
- allowing the child more time to process the letters and sounds learnt in order to blend and read a word;
- ensuring adults are speaking clearly in front of the child so they can watch the shape of their mouth as they speak. This is known as lip-reading but shouldn't be relied on as the only way for a child to understand speech as many sounds and words look alike;
- using a multisensory approach.

Criticisms

No educational approach can be a one-size-fits-all, and this is true of systematic synthetic phonics. There has been criticism of SSP when it comes to children with certain SEND.

Evidence does show us that SSP is one of the best ways to teach children to read (DfE, 2023c). However, organisations such as the British Dyslexia Association (BDA) argue that SSP should not be promoted by the DfE as the only way to teach children to read, as it has limitations, which means that children with dyslexia may benefit from a range of strategies alongside SSP (BDA, 2021). As practitioners, we should always be evaluating the needs of the children in our care and assessing the best way we can support them. For some children this may mean using multiple approaches when teaching reading, along with an SSP programme.

Conclusion

Knowing how to support children with a special educational need or disability should be a priority for all practitioners working with young people. We want phonics to be as accessible and inclusive as possible, to allow all children to achieve the outcomes they are capable of. Having high expectations of children of all abilities means they will receive appropriate challenge at their own level of development. It is also important to remember that children with, for example, neurodiversity have strengths as well as challenges. All children are unique, and an individualised approach should be taken for all children, while working with families and the SENDCo to plan for effective support.

8
Working with Parents and Carers

This chapter will cover:

1. the importance of parent/carer involvement;
2. common misconceptions parents/carers have about phonics;
3. barriers to parent/carer involvement;
4. how to encourage parent/carer involvement;
5. how to hold a phonics workshop for parents and carers.

Introduction

There is only so much we as practitioners can do for and with children during the hours they are in our care. The home–school or home–setting connection is extremely important for all aspects of a child's education and wellbeing, as families and settings should be working as a team to 'effect mutual support and shared values' (Desforges, 2003).

Parent/carer involvement has a positive impact on children's progress and outcomes. Therefore, we should seek to create a good rapport with families to surround the child with positive influences, support and modelling. When it comes to phonics, parents and carers often need support themselves to understand how phonics works.

Common misconceptions for parents and carers

Parents and carers not understanding phonics is precisely the reason that the Little Learners Education YouTube channel was created; to support parents and carers in learning about phonics and how best to support their children with phonics and reading at home. Some parents and carers can feel embarrassed about not understanding phonics and not knowing how to support their child with their reading, so it is important to address misconceptions with sensitivity and patience.

The most common misconception for parents and carers is usually the use of the *schwa*. When the majority of parents and carers were at school and learning to read, phonics was taught quite differently, or not at all. Children were commonly taught letter sounds with schwas, leading many parents and carers to believe that letters like l, m and s are pronounced 'luh' 'muh' and 'suh'. Even with the best of intentions, which most parents and carers will have, this misunderstanding of how to pronounce sounds can cause confusion for children and even lead to children mispronouncing sounds they have already learnt. This in turn can result in difficulty when blending.

For some parents and carers, phonics may be a completely new concept to them, having been taught to read using rote learning and learning by sight. These parents and carers may believe that reading is more about memorisation or be intimidated by the world of phonics.

Barriers to parent/carer involvement

Parent/carer involvement continues to be a difficult concept for a number of reasons. First of all, practitioners are trained very little in working with parents and carers, if at all. It is up to settings to make sure staff understand how to reach out to families and encourage a safe and welcoming environment for them. Settings should have policies in place to help facilitate positive home–setting relationships.

In a 2021 parent survey it was found that the top barrier to parent/carer involvement was 'time'. The second highest barrier was 'simply not being asked' (Parentkind, 2021).

If we as practitioners can understand the barriers parents and carers may face when trying to engage with phonics, we can work to bridge the gap and encourage families to support their child's education. After all, most parents and carers do want to do so, but don't know how. '[P]arents with a low level of belief in their ability to help their children are likely to avoid contact with schools because of their view that such involvement will not bring about positive outcomes for their children' (Hornby and Lafaele, 2011, p. 40). Parents and carers may feel embarrassed, intimidated or anxious about approaching a school or setting for help with phonics (or another area of learning).

Factors such as not speaking English or speaking little English can impact a parent/carer's relationship with both the setting and with phonics. It can be daunting to communicate with the setting if an interpreter is not provided, or letters home aren't written in the parent/carer's native language. Imagine then, trying to support their own child with phonics in a language they cannot speak. This could be frustrating and, while the desire to support their child is strong, their ability to do so may be limited. Similarly, parents and carers who are illiterate face similar challenges. In the UK, 18 per cent of adults have 'very poor literacy skills' (National Literacy Trust, n.d.).

For parents and carers with English as an additional language (EAL), it is still important to share stories, sing songs and talk in their first language. This allows children to develop their communication skills and enjoy reading and storytelling at home, as well as strengthen the pride children have for their own culture. Using audiobooks or ebooks can be helpful when sharing books in English, so the child hears the English words and can read along and still gets to share this with the parent/carer. If the parent/carer is learning or improving their own English skills, this can be a lovely way to share in that learning together.

Of course, many parents and carers with EAL do not learn English and there are still many ways they can be involved in their child's phonics and reading, as can parents and carers with poor literacy skills. Settings can offer individualised support and activities for families to try at home, which suit the parent/carer's confidence with English and reading; this may involve bilingual resources, picture clues or simple instructions that the practitioner can explain before they are taken home. In these cases, phonics videos such as those on the @LittleLearnersVideos YouTube channel can be helpful for parents and carers to use at home.

A parent/carer's own level and experience of education, home responsibilities (such as having multiple dependants or caring for an elderly relative), medical concerns and learning difficulties of their own can all have an impact on how they interact with their child's school or setting. While a child's education is certainly a shared responsibility, 'teachers are nowadays ... working in an environment where they are increasingly held accountable for children's achievements' (Hornby and Lafaele, 2011, p. 46). The education children receive at home and the environment they live in play a crucial role in their development and progress, which should be communicated to parents and carers. Settings should emphasise the role the parents and carers play in their child's education and how important they are as part of their child's learning journey.

Ideas for supporting parents/carers

Expecting parents and carers to engage with phonics at home with their children is pointless if settings do not offer support for parents and carers on the topic. Below are some ideas of how to help parents and carers with phonics and to give them confidence when supporting their child:

- *workshops*: offer phonics workshops for parents and carers so they can learn and ask questions. It is best to offer a workshop at the beginning of the academic year, if that is appropriate for your setting. Follow-up sessions can be offered later on, particularly when a new phase is being entered (for example, explaining digraphs for Phase Three);
- *weekly information sheets*: these can be sent home at the end of each week. The sheet should include the sounds children have learnt that week and how to pronounce them. It can also list various words children are learning to read (for example, CVC words) which parents and carers can go through with their child. Tricky words may also be included, with an explanation of how these should be read (by sight, not sounded out). It is also helpful to add contact information for a practitioner who can offer further support for parents and carers who need it;
- *videos*: signpost parents and carers to videos which show how to pronounce each sound and how to decode words. You can find videos for this on the Little Learners Education YouTube channel, @LittleLearnersVideos. This can give parents and carers the opportunity to learn in their own time and in their own space;
- *drop-in sessions*: offer times when parents and carers can come in to see a practitioner to discuss phonics and any problems they are having with reading at home. Sometimes the reassurance that they are doing the right thing, or advice on how to do something, is all a parent/carer needs to feel more confident when helping their child;
- *flexibility*: offer some flexibility for parents and carers to contact the setting to discuss their child's phonics journey. This could be offering an out-of-hours session or using video calls for parents and carers who have difficulty coming in for a face-to-face meeting;
- *encourage reading for the whole family*: tell parents and carers about the importance of children seeing their parents/carers reading, whether this is a newspaper,

magazine or book. Modelling this behaviour allows children to see that reading for pleasure can be part of their everyday life, even as adults;
- *encourage shared reading*: explain to parents and carers that books can be read to, with and by their children. Reading aloud to children models how fluency can sound and allows the child to be immersed in the story. Reading together gives children the opportunity to join in, sharing a book with an adult;
- *technology*: for many families, their economic background makes accessing technology like laptops, computers or tablets difficult or impossible. It can be helpful for your setting to offer times for parents and carers to come in and use this technology with their children, playing phonics games together in a different way than they are able to at home. This can make phonics learning more accessible for a variety of children and their families;
- *parent/carer helpers*: invite parents and carers to come into the setting for an hour or so to help with the running of the setting and to support children. This can allow parents and carers to see how phonics is taught and modelled throughout the setting and provision, as well as make them feel more involved and strengthen the relationship between them and the setting;
- *regular check-ins* with parents and carers of children with SEND.

Example workshop

Giving a workshop to parents and carers doesn't have to be complicated. It is best to keep things simple, with a clear structure, so as to not overwhelm anyone. Allow parents and carers to ask questions during the session, or, if they prefer, speak with you afterwards about any concerns or queries. It's best to have an informal and relaxed environment.

Ensure all parents and carers are invited to the session and given a fair amount of notice. It can be helpful to upload any presentation slides, or even a video of the session, to a platform parents and carers who cannot attend the session can access.

In this example, the phonics workshop is introducing Phase Two phonics. When giving the workshop, make sure you include:

- *what phonics is*: a summary of systematic synthetic phonics and why we teach phonics in this structured way;
- *a brief summary* of Phase One phonics, which children will have been engaging with up until this point;

- *what children will be learning*: the sounds (in order), segmenting and blending;
- *information* about the phonics scheme you are using;
- *the correct pronunciations* of sounds, including misuse of the schwa;
- *how to engage* with phonics at home with a few examples of games to play and the importance of reading together;
- *a chance to play* some of the games/engage in the activities recommended for home;
- *phonics-specific language*: words like 'phoneme', 'grapheme', 'decoding', 'segmenting' and 'blending' are important for parents and carers to know, as children may be using these words;
- *allow time for any questions*;
- *give a handout* for parents and carers to take home with some of the key points from the session.

The example above can be adjusted to suit the phase of phonics children are learning. For example, for Phase Three, there should be an explanation of digraphs and how to decode words that contain them. For Phase Five, the workshop should concentrate on alternative pronunciations and spellings, and how to support children when they come across these in their reading.

Conclusion

Working together with parents, carers and families is imperative to give children the best chance to progress. Creating a community in which parents and carers feel involved in school/setting life and feel confident to ask questions allows for a close relationship between settings and families. Reaching some parents and carers can be difficult due to some of the barriers mentioned, but knowing what these barriers can be allows practitioners to identify them and put the relevant support in place. The opportunity to be involved in their child's education should be as accessible and inclusive as possible for parents and carers. Giving parents and carers the information they need about phonics empowers them to further support their child and continue their phonics learning at home. Parental involvement improves achievement and outcomes, so as practitioners we should aim to accomplish this for as many children as possible.

9
Further Support

This chapter will cover:

1. how to find support using Little Learners Education;
2. official documents to refer to;
3. continuing professional development;
4. other websites and apps that can support phonics learning;
5. how to contact me.

There are so many places to find further support and guidance on the topic of phonics! Of course, this book can be your first go-to for phonics advice. However, if you're looking for some specific documents, videos to support your understanding or somewhere to connect with other practitioners, the list below can help.

Little Learners Education

My company, Little Learners Education, was created with phonics in mind! After a while I branched out to other areas of learning, but phonics has always been and will always be my passion. It's no wonder then, that both my website and YouTube channel have loads of phonics guidance and resources to support you.

- *YouTube.com/LittleLearnersVideos*
  - My YouTube channel, @LittleLearnersVideos, has over 100 videos about phonics, both for practitioners and for students. You can hear how each letter sound should be pronounced, watch how I structure phonics lessons, learn a variety of phonics activities and how to carry them out, and even find videos to use with the children in your care.
  - The comments section of videos is also a great place to look for answers to questions or suggestions from other practitioners from around the world! We have built a wonderful community on the Little Learners YouTube channel, and it is helpful to learn from others and share practice.
- *LittleLearners.Education*
  - My website, littlelearners.education, has phonics guides with videos attached to give you an in-depth look at different areas of phonics. I also have downloadable resources available, including *phonics packs* for each phase and *lanyard cards* for practitioners in the EYFS. You can also find links to my CPD courses and information about how to book consultations with me.
- *Social media*
  - You can find me on Instagram and Facebook as @LittleLearnersVideos, sharing information about phonics, other areas of the EYFS and advice for parents and carers.

Documents

We have referred to a lot of different documents in this book, many of which have been published by the DfE. Below is a list of those you may wish to take a look at:

- *Early Years Foundation Stage Framework* (2024b)
- *Early Years Foundation Stage Profile Handbook* (2024c)
- *Development Matters* (2023a)
- *National Curriculum in England: Primary Curriculum* (2013)
- *Letters and Sounds: Principles and Practice of High Quality Phonics* (2007)

- *The Reading Framework* (2023c)
- *Choosing a Phonics Teaching Programme* (2024a)
- *Phonics Screening Check: 2023 and 2024 Materials* (2023b and 2024d)

Another document I find particularly useful is *Birth to 5 Matters*, by the Early Years Coalition (2021).

Continuing professional development

As practitioners, we are always learning and evolving our practice. As new research comes to light and teaching methods change, it is important that we stay informed about how to best support the children in our care. In terms of phonics, there are certain CPD courses you may wish to partake in:

- *training offered by your local authority*: these can be set courses or bespoke for your setting and the needs of practitioners;
- *online courses, including mine!* Each of my CPD courses end with a certificate of completion for you to add to your CPD records. You can find more information about these courses on my website, littlelearners.education;
- *scheme-specific training*: it can be helpful to receive training from the company supplying your setting's phonics scheme to ensure you understand how it aligns with the fundamentals of phonics and the way children are expected to learn with that particular scheme.

Classroom resources

There are so many websites and apps that offer phonics games and activities for practitioners to use with their students. Little Learners Education (@LittleLearnersVideos on YouTube) videos and playlists can help with children's understanding of new sounds, revising sounds learnt and decoding words. There are entire playlists of 'Segmenting and blending' and 'Phonics lessons' which can be helpful for practitioners to use with their children.

Other websites and apps that I have found particularly useful include:

- Twinkl.co.uk – thousands of resources including phonics games, activities and planning;
- PinkCatGames.com – a range of games to play for which you can make your own word lists (I would recommend this rather than selecting pre-made word lists);

- PhonicsBloom.com – interactive games and resources;
- Alphablocks World – an app which features the popular BBC Alphablocks, progressing through the phonics phases with games and decodable stories;
- Alphablocks Letter Fun – another app featuring the BBC Alphablocks with minigames;
- Teach your monster to read – an app which progresses through the phonics phases using engaging activities and a fun avatar to take children through their phonics journey.

Contact me

My inbox is always open! If you have questions or want to book a consultation, you can contact me using the following:

Email: amy@littlelearners.education

Instagram: @LittleLearnersVideos

Facebook: @LittleLearnersVideos

Final thoughts

Phonics really is incredible. As practitioners, we are able to support children as their communication skills grow and eventually teach them to read and write. What an enormous privilege! I don't think I will ever stop loving this area of education.

Phonics is a gateway to so much: being able to interact with others, reading to find information or to escape into imaginary worlds, write and share ideas … it's never-ending. Without the vital skills phonics teaches, children are unable to access a great deal of other learning.

Next time you are supporting a child with their phonics, remember: this is important. In this moment, you have the power to unlock a world of opportunities, experiences and information for that child. What could be more rewarding than that?

Jargon buster glossary

There is so much phonics-specific vocabulary – as well as other jargon related to teaching phonics – that you can certainly be forgiven for not knowing every word, or even forgetting something you once knew. When moving between phases and teaching different ages, it is natural to want a bit of a refresher. Here, you will find all of those words, phrases and more, along with their definitions.

Adjacent consonants

Two or three consonants next to each other in a word. For example, the 'lk' in 'milk' or the 'str' in 'string'.

Aspects

The sections of Phase One phonics. There are seven aspects within Phase One phonics:

- Aspect 1: general sound discrimination – environmental sounds
- Aspect 2: general sound discrimination – instrumental sounds
- Aspect 3: general sound discrimination – body percussion
- Aspect 4: rhythm and rhyme
- Aspect 5: alliteration
- Aspect 6: voice sounds
- Aspect 7: oral segmenting and blending.

Assessment

A method of evaluating a child's progress or level of development.

Blend/blending

Bringing sounds/phonemes together in order to then read the whole word.

CCVC word

Consonant – consonant – vowel – consonant word. For example: 'swing'.

Child-led

Learning that follows children's own interests and allows them to choose what activity they will engage with and how they will interact with it.

Common-exception words

Words that do not follow the usual spelling rules of the English language, but are still commonly used. Examples include 'the', 'go' and 'some'.

Compound words

Two or more words that when brought together make a new word with its own meaning. For example, 'foot' and 'ball' come together to create 'football'. There are three types of compound word:

- *closed*: two words that have come together to make one new word with a new meaning. Examples include 'sunflower', 'breakfast' and 'snowball'.
- *open*: two words that create a new meaning together but are still separated by a space and appear as two words. Examples include: 'post office', 'living room' and 'full moon'.
- *hyphenated*: two words connected by a hyphen to create a new meaning. Examples include: 'one-sided', 'mother-in-law' and 'close-up'.

Consonant

Letter sounds, created by obstructing the breath in the vocal tract when saying them. The consonants of the English language are: b, c, d, f, g, h, j, k, l, m, n, p, q(u), r, s, t, v, w, x, y, z.

Consonant blend

Two or more adjacent consonants that each retain their own individual sounds, rather than becoming a digraph or trigraph (for which a new sound is created). Examples of consonant blends include 'tw' in 'twig', 'dr' in 'drink'' and 'spr' in 'spring'.

Consonant digraph

Two consonants that come together to make one sound. Examples of consonant digraphs include 'sh' such as in 'ship', 'ch' such as in 'chat' and 'th' such as in 'teeth'.

Continuous provision

The resources, learning spaces and activities that children have access to at all times, encouraging independence, exploration and learning through play.

Contraction

The shortened form of two or more words, where the omitted letters are replaced by an apostrophe. Examples of contractions include 'do not' becoming 'don't', 'I am' becoming 'I'm' and 'could not have' becoming 'couldn't've'.

Curriculum

A course of study outlining the subjects and subject matter that should be taught.

CVC word

Consonant – vowel – consonant word. Examples of CVC words include 'cat', 'man' and 'log'.

CVCC word

Consonant – vowel – consonant – consonant word. Examples of CVCC words include 'milk', 'desk' and 'tent'.

Decode

Sounding out a word to be able to read it, using segmenting and blending skills.

DfE

Department for Education. This is a department of the government responsible for 'children's services and education including Early Years, schools, higher and further education policy, apprenticeships and wider skills in England' (DfE, n.d.).

Digraph

Two letters that come together to make one sound. Examples of digraphs include 'ai' in 'rain', 'ng' in 'swing' and 'sh' in 'shop'.

Differentiation

Adapting teaching and learning to cater to individual needs.

Early learning goals (ELGs)

The ELGs are a set of 17 statements that reflect the expected level of development by the end of the Reception year in each area of learning. Children are assessed against the ELGs at the end of their Reception year and this assessment is used in the Early Years Foundation Stage profile.

Early Years Foundation Stage (EYFS) profile

The EYFS profile is a statutory assessment that takes place at the end of the Reception year (or the academic year in which a child turns five). A child's level of development is assessed against the ELGs and practitioners must assess whether or not a child meets the expected level of development. Children are given a level of either *expected* for working at the expected level of development, or *emerging* for still working towards the expected level of development. The purpose of the profile is to provide a summative assessment at the end of the EYFS, to inform practitioners in Year 1 of a child's level of development and to aid the transition from Reception to Year 1.

End sound

The last sound in a word. Examples include /g/ in 'dog', /ch/ in 'bench' and /x/ in 'lunchbox'.

EYFS

Early Years Foundation Stage. This is the stage of learning and care for children from birth to age five.

EYFS Framework

The *EYFS Framework* (DfE, 2024a) is the set of standards that all Early Years providers must adhere to. The *Framework* also includes the areas of learning and expectations for development to ensure children reach the expected level of development by age five.

Free-flow

A style of learning environment which allows children to freely move between indoor and outdoor areas, choosing the resources and activities they want to engage with through play-based learning.

Formative assessment

A method of ongoing evaluation which informs feedback, planning, teaching and learning in real time.

GPC

Grapheme–phoneme correspondence. For example, the grapheme 'd' makes the /d/ sound in 'dog', and the grapheme 'ch' makes the /ch/ sound in 'chip'.

Grapheme

A written letter or group of letters. Graphemes are used to represent phonemes.

High-frequency words

Words that appear very frequently in the English language when reading. This includes words such as 'a', 'the' and 'when'. Being able to read these words allows children to become more fluent and confident readers.

Initial sound

The first sound/phoneme in a word. For example, the initial sound in 'frog' is /f/ and the initial sound in 'think' is /th/.

KS1

Key Stage 1. This is the first stage of primary education under the national curriculum and covers Year 1 and Year 2.

KS2

Key Stage 2. This is the second and final stage of primary education under the national curriculum and covers Year 3, Year 4, Year 5 and Year 6.

Long vowel sound

A vowel sound that is pronounced in the same way as its name in the alphabet. For example, the 'a' in 'acorn' is making the long /ai/ sound rather than the short /a/ sound. We also have digraphs that make long vowel sounds, such as the 'oo' in 'moon' making the long /oo/ sound, rather than the short /oo/ sound such as in 'book'.

Loose parts

Items or objects that have no particular purpose and can be used alone or with other items in a variety of ways.

Magic e

The magic e refers to the letter 'e' at the end of a split digraph. This 'magic e' can make the vowel before it say its name, like in 'cake' or 'home'. This is another way of teaching the concept of a split digraph.

Monosyllabic

A word made up of one syllable, such as 'sun', 'lake' or 'swing'.

National curriculum

The national curriculum is a set of subjects and standards used by primary and secondary schools which ensures consistency in what children learn across all schools. It provides guidance on the subjects to be taught, and the standards children should reach in each subject throughout primary and secondary school.

Open-ended activity

An activity which does not have a predetermined or expected outcome but rather encourages children to interact in whatever way they want to, using their imagination, exploration, independence and problem-solving skills.

Pedagogy

The theory and practice of teaching, understanding what allows children to develop and using this to inform teaching methods.

Phases

Each stage of synthetic systematic phonics. There are six phases of phonics, each building on the skills from the previous stage to support children in their communication and language skills, reading and writing.

Phoneme

The smallest unit of sound. Phonemes are the sounds letters/graphemes make. For example, the grapheme 'w' makes the /w/ phoneme in 'web', and the grapheme 'ai' makes the /ai/ phoneme in 'rain'. There are four phonemes in the word 'crab' – /c/ /r/ /a/ /b/ – and three phonemes in the word 'teeth' – /t/ /ee/ /th/.

Phoneme frame

A grid made of boxes next to each other to help children write a word by showing how many phonemes are needed.

Phonics

Phonics is the method of teaching reading and writing that focuses on the relationship between graphemes (written letters) and phonemes (sounds), known as grapheme–phoneme correspondence (GPC).

Phonics screening check

The phonics screening check is a statutory assessment which assesses a child's decoding skills, using real words and pseudo-words (known as 'alien words'). This assessment takes place in Year 1, although some children may take or retake the check in Year 2.

Polysyllabic

A word made up of two or more syllables, such as 'farmer', 'beautiful' and 'caterpillar'.

Practitioner

An adult involved in the education of children, such as a teacher, teaching assistant, childminder or nursery practitioner.

Provision

The environment, resources, activities and opportunities children have access to.

Quadgraph

A sound represented by four letters, such as /ough/ in 'through'.

Reception

The final year of the EYFS. Children attend Reception in the academic year that they turn five. This is usually seen as the first formal year of school, with most Reception classes being in primary schools.

Scaffolding

Support given to a child when learning a new skill, which is gradually reduced over time as the child's development progresses and their understanding meets the appropriate level for a particular task.

Schwa

The utterance 'uh' – in phonics, we refer to the schwa as the 'uh' sound being spoken when it is not needed. This can lead to the mispronunciation of sounds and words. For example, adding a schwa to the /m/ sound makes it sound like 'muh', which is the incorrect pronunciation for that letter.

Segment/segmenting

Breaking up a word into its smallest units of sound (phonemes). For example, the word 'garden' can be segmented into /g/ /ar/ /d/ /e/ /n/.

Setting

The environment or location where education is taking place. Children in the EYFS may be in a school setting, nursery, preschool, childminder or a variety of other Early Years settings.

Short vowel sound

The sound a vowel makes when it is not elongated. For example, the 'a' in 'cat' makes the /a/ sound. We also have short vowel digraph sounds, such as the /oo/ in 'cook' rather than the /oo/ in 'food'.

Sight words

Words that children learn by sight because they are high-frequency words. These may be decodable or not decodable. Sight words may include words such as 'the', 'mum' or 'little'.

Sound buttons

Dots and lines placed under a word to show whether a sound in a word is represented by one or more letters. For single grapheme sounds, we use a dot. For digraphs and trigraphs, we use lines.

Sound out

A way of saying 'decode'; to segment and blend to read a word.

Split digraph

A digraph – two letters making one sound – where the graphemes in the digraphs are separated by another grapheme. For example, 'a_e' in 'bake' or 'i_e' in 'pine'.

Summative assessment

A method of evaluating a child's learning at the end of a period of time (for example, the end of a topic, term or year) to find out what they can recall from what they have learnt, and the level of development they are working at.

Systematic synthetic phonics

The method we use to teach children to read, by matching sounds to their corresponding written letters, in a structured way, to put those sounds together and read whole words.

Tricky words

Words that cannot be decoded using phonics. These are also known as common-exception words as they do not use the typical rules of spelling.

Trigraph

Three letters that come together to make one sound. Examples of trigraphs include 'igh' in 'night' and 'air' in 'chair'.

VC word

Vowel–consonant words. Examples include 'it', 'at' and 'on'.

Vowel

A letter sound, the air of which when spoken is not obstructed. The vowels of the English language are: a, e, i, o and u, with 'y' also sometimes being used as a vowel in words such as 'my' (/igh/ sound) and 'funny' (/ee/ sound).

Vowel digraph

Two vowels that come together to make one sound. Examples of vowel digraphs include the 'ai' in 'train' and the 'ee' in 'three'.

References

Aphantasia Network (2019) *What is Aphantasia?* Available at: https://aphantasia.com/what-is-aphantasia/ (accessed 19 February 2025).

Arciuli, J. and Bailey, B. (2021) The promise of comprehensive early reading instruction for children with autism and recommendations for future directions. *Language, Speech, and Hearing Services in Schools*, 52(1), 225–38. https://doi.org/10.1044/2020_LSHSS-20-00019

Autistica (n.d.) *Autistic Strengths*. Available at: www.autistica.org.uk/what-is-autism/autistic-strengths (accessed 7 April 2025).

British Dyslexia Association (BDA) (2021) *Systematic, Synthetic Phonics (SSP): Help Us Make a Change. Sign Our Petition*. Available at: www.bdadyslexia.org.uk/news/systematic-synthetic-phonics-ssp-help-us-make-a-change-sign-our-petition (accessed 9 April 2025).

BDA (n.d.) *About Dyslexia*. Available at: www.bdadyslexia.org.uk/dyslexia/about-dyslexia (accessed 7 April 2025).

Campbell, T. and Kelly, J. (2024) *What can Quantitative Analyses Tell Us About the National Impact of the Phonics Screening Check?* Education Policy Institute. Available at: https://epi.org.uk/publications-and-research/what-can-quantitative-analyses-tell-us-about-the-national-impact-of-the-phonics-screening-check/ (accessed 22 April 2025).

Department for Education (DfE) (2007) *Letters and Sounds: Principles and Practice of High Quality Phonics*. Available at: https://assets.publishing.service.gov.uk/media/67124a19b40d67191077b36e/Letters_and_Sounds_-_Phase_One.pdf (accessed 21 May 2025).

DfE (2013) *National Curriculum in England*. Available at: www.gov.uk/government/collections/national-curriculum (accessed 22 April 2025).

DfE (2021) *Teachers' Standards*. Available at: https://assets.publishing.service.gov.uk/media/61b73d6c8fa8f50384489c9a/Teachers__Standards_Dec_2021.pdf (accessed 23 May 2025).

DfE (2023a) *Development Matters*. Available at: https://assets.publishing.service.gov.uk/media/64e6002a20ae890014f26cbc/DfE_Development_Matters_Report_Sep2023.pdf (accessed 26 May 2025).

DfE (2023b) *Phonics Screening Check: Key Stage 1*. Available at: https://assets.publishing.service.gov.uk/media/6495b5d7831311 00132962d0/2023_phonics_pupils_materials_standard.pdf (accessed 26 May 2025).

DfE (2023c) *The Reading Framework*. Available at: www.gov.uk/government/publications/the-reading-framework-teaching-the-foundations-of-literacy (accessed 22 April 2025).

DfE (2024a) *Choosing a Phonics Teaching Programme*. Available at: www.gov.uk/government/publications/choosing-a-phonics-teaching-programme/list-of-phonics-teaching-programmes (accessed 22 April 2025).

DfE (2024b) *Early Years Foundation Stage (EYFS) Statutory Framework*. Available at: www.gov.uk/government/publications/early-years-foundation-stage-framework–2 (accessed 22 April 2025).

DfE (2024c) *Early Years Foundation Stage Profile Handbook*. Available at: https://assets.publishing.service.gov.uk/media/6747436ba72d7eb7f348c08b/Early_years_foundation_stage_profile_handbook.pdf (accessed 26 May 2025).

DfE (2024d) *Phonics Screening Check: 2024 Materials*. Available at: www.gov.uk/government/publications/phonics-screening-check-2024-materials (accessed 26 May 2025).

DfE (n.d.) *Department for Education*. Available at: www.gov.uk/government/organisations/department-for-education (accessed 2 April 2025).

Desforges, C. (2003) *The Impact of Parental Involvement, Parental Support and Family Education on Pupil Achievement and Adjustment: A Literature Review*. Available at: www.nationalnumeracy.org.uk/sites/default/files/documents/impact_of_parental_involvement/the_impact_of_parental_involvement.pdf (accessed 24 April 2025).

Donaldson, J. and Scheffler, A. (1999) *The Gruffalo*. London: Macmillan.

Early Years Coalition (EYC) (2021) *Birth to 5 Matters: Learning Environments*. Available at: https://birthto5matters.org.uk/ (accessed 22 April 2025).

Guardian (2006) Q&A: synthetic phonics. *Guardian*. Available at: www.theguardian.com/education/2006/mar/20/schools.uk (accessed 22 April 2025).

Ginnis, S., Pestell, E., Mason, E. and Knibbs, S. (2018) *Newly Qualified Teachers: Annual Survey 2017*. Digital Education Resource Archive (DERA). Available at: https://dera.ioe.ac.uk/id/eprint/32135/ (accessed 22 April 2025).

Hardach, S. (2023) Why do some people mirror write? *BBC Future*. Available at: www.bbc.co.uk/future/article/20230405-why-do-some-people-mirror-write (accessed 24 January 2025).

Hornby, G. and Lafaele, R. (2011) Barriers to parental involvement in education: an explanatory model. *Educational Review*, 63(1), 37–52. Available at: www.tandfonline.com/doi/abs/10.1080/00131911.2010.488049 (accessed 24 April 2025).

Jolly Learning (1987) *Jolly Phonics*. Available at: https://jollylearning.com/jolly-phonics (accessed 22 April 2025).

MacKenzie, L. Bailey, G. and Turton, D. (2016) *Our Dialects: Mapping Variation in English in the UK*. Available at: www.ourdialects.uk/about/ (accessed 2 February 2025).

Miskin, R. (2002) *Read, Write, Inc*. Available at: www.ruthmiskin.com/ (accessed 22 April 2025).

Musician's Union (2018) *Access to Music Lessons Dying out for Poorer Families*. Available at: https://musiciansunion.org.uk/news/access-to-music-lessons-dying-out-for-poorer-families (accessed 2 January 2025).

National Deaf Children's Society (NDCS) (2021) *Information about deaf children and young people in the UK*. Available at: www.ndcs.org.uk/media/6809/dcyp-in-the-uk-info-sheet.pdf (accessed 15 March 2025).

NDCS (2025) *Glue Ear*. Available at: www.ndcs.org.uk/documents-and-resources/glue-ear-a-guide-for-parents/ (accessed 15 March 2025).

National Literacy Trust (n.d.) *Adult Literacy*. Available at: https://literacytrust.org.uk/parents-and-families/adult-literacy/ (accessed 24 April 2025).

NHS (n.d.) *Early Learning and Development*. Available at: www.nhs.uk/start-for-life/early-learning-development/ (accessed 13 March 2025).

Online Etymology Dictionary (n.d.) *Origin and history of 'beige'*. Available at: www.etymonline.com/word/beige (accessed 17 February 2025).

Nordby, E.S., Guribye, F., Nordgreen, T. and Lundervold, A.J. (2023) Silver linings of ADHD: a thematic analysis of adults' positive experiences with living with ADHD. *BMJ Open*. Available at: https://bmjopen.bmj.com/content/13/10/e072052 (accessed 28 May 2025).

Parentkind (2021) *Parent Voice Report 2021*. Available at: www.parentkind.org.uk/assets/resources/Parent-Voice-Report-2021.pdf (accessed 24 April 2025).

Propio (2023) *What Makes English Such a Difficult Language to Learn?* Available at: https://propio.com/2023/10/28/what-makes-english-such-a-difficult-language-to-learn/(accessed: 17 March 2025).

Sriram, R. (2020) Why ages 2–7 matter so much for brain development. *Edutopia*. Available at: www.edutopia.org/article/why-ages-2-7-matter-so-much-brain-development/ (accessed 16 March 2025).

Standards and Testing Agency (2025a) *National Curriculum Assessments: Past Test Materials.* Available at: www.gov.uk/government/collections/national-curriculum-assessments-past-test-materials (accessed 22 April 2025).

Standards and Testing Agency (2025b) *Phonics Screening Check Administration Guidance.* Available at: www.gov.uk/government/publications/key-stage-1-phonics-screening-check-administration-guidance/2024-phonics-screening-check-administration-guidance (accessed 16 March 2025).

Tayler, V. (2023) *Regional Accents and Phonics: Should You Change Your Accent for Phonics?* Available at: www.twinkl.co.uk/news/regional-accents-and-phonics-ks1-digest (accessed 22 April 2025).

YouGov (2019) *Teachers' Awareness and Perceptions of Ofsted.* Teacher Attitude Survey 2019 Report. Available at: https://assets.publishing.service.gov.uk/media/5d5a57aa40f0b6706a2c5696/Teacher_Attitude_Survey_2019_report.pdf (accessed: 22 April 2025).

Index

accents
   Phase Two, 39
   Phase Three, 50–51
   Phase Five, 69
activities
   Phase One (for aspect 1)
      listening walk, 17
      our favourite sounds, 18
      sound hide and seek, 17–18
   Phase One (for aspect 2)
      noise makers, 20
      story sounds, 19
      what's that instrument?, 19
   Phase One (for aspect 3)
      action songs/rhymes, 22
      copy me, 21
      pass it on, 21
   Phase One (for aspect 4)
      clapping syllables, 22
      odd one out, 22
      rhyming books, 22
   Phase One (for aspect 5)
      alliterative sentences, 24
      I spy, 24
      what's in my sound bag?, 24
   Phase One (for aspect 6)
      can you make your voice do this?, 25
      watch your sounds, 25
      whose voice is that?, 26
   Phase One (for aspect 7)
      find the object, 26
      I spy with segmenting, 27
      sound out and run, 27
   Phase Two (for introducing new phonemes and graphemes)
      making graphemes with natural objects, 33
      objects in small-world play or role play, 32
      outdoor grapheme hunt, 33
      searching for sounds in messy play, 33
      tray game, 32

   Phase Two (for specific sounds)
      /b/ buttons, 36
      /c/ caterpillar, 36
      /d/ digging for dinosaurs, 36
      /f/ finding fairies, 37
      glittery /g/, 36
      /m/ animals, 35
      popping bubbles for /p/, 35
      /r/ rocks, 36
      the /s/ café, 35
   Phase Two (for CVC words)
      CVC puzzles, 38
      missing initial sound, 38
      word hunt, 38
   Phase Two (for tricky words)
      feed the puppet, 41
      finding tricky words in books, 41
      matching tricky words, 41
      tricky word hunt, 40
   Phase Three
      digraph treasure, 49
      Duplo™ CVC words, 50
      fishing for digraphs, 50
      matching digraphs, 49
      playdough sound buttons, 50
   Phase Three (for tricky words)
      splat the tricky word, 52
      spot and dot, 52–53
      tricky words in books, 53
   Phase Four (for CCVC and CVCC words)
      giant chalk words, 56
      listen and frame, 55
      word fix, 55
   Phase Five
      grapheme clock, 68
      magic 'e' game, 68
      mirror words, 69
      phoneme finder, 66–67
      phonics peg wheel, 67–68
      rare spellings, 67

Phase Six
  present to past tense, 72
  rare GPC sentences, 73
  spelling pattern investigation, 72–73
  word builder, 73
phonics screening check
  alien word bingo, 88
  astronaut words, 87
  Dog and Quog, 86–87
  LittleLearnersVideos YouTube video, 88
  name that alien, 88
  past papers, 88
  stepping stones, 87
adjacent consonants, 121
alien words, 7, 81, 86–88, 91–93, 128
alliteration, 23–24
Alphablocks Letter Fun, 120
Alphablocks World, 120
aspects (seven), within Phase One phonics, 16–27, 121
assessment
  Phase One, 28
  Phase Two, 41–42
  Phase Three, 53
  Phase Four, 57–58
  Phase Five, 70
  Phase Six, 76
attention deficit hyperactivity disorder (ADHD), 107
autism, 104–105

blending, 8, 122. *See also* segmenting and blending
body percussion, 20–22
book corner, 99–100
British Dyslexia Association (BDA), 109

CCVC words, 54–56, 122
'chunking', 57
classroom resources, 119–120
closed compound words, 57, 122
common-exception words. *See* tricky words
compound words, 56–57, 122
comprehension skills, 75–76
consonant blends, 123
consonant digraphs, 44, 82, 123
consonants, 123
continuing professional development (CPD) courses, 119
continuous past tense, 72
continuous provision, 123
  in EYFS, 96–97
  in Key Stage 1, 97
contractions, 123
cued speech, 90
curriculum, 123

CVC (consonant–vowel–consonant) words, 26, 30, 124
  with digraphs, 48
  segmenting and blending, 37–38
CVCC words, 54–56, 124

deafness, 107–109
decoding skills, 81, 86, 92, 102, 128
decoding words, 8, 37, 119, 124
Department for Education (DfE), 3, 5, 9–10, 71, 91, 100, 118, 124
differentiation, 124
digraphs, 7, 44, 46, 48, 124
dyslexia, 105–106

early career teacher (ECT), 1
  programme, 3
early learning goals (ELGs), 124
Early Years Foundation Stage (EYFS), 3–4, 100
  continuous provision in, 96
  EYFS Framework, 125
  EYFS profile, 125
Education Policy Institute (EPI), 92
enabling environments, 98–100
end sound, 125
environmental sounds, 16–18

formative assessment, 126
'free-flow', 96, 125

grapheme–phoneme correspondence (GPC), 44, 71, 73, 84, 91, 126, 128
graphemes, 29, 30–33, 60–62, 126

hearing loss and deafness, 107–109
high-frequency words, 39, 82, 126
hyphenated compound words, 57, 122

initial sound, 126
instrumental sounds, 18–20
instruments, 100

Jolly Phonics, 6, 34

Key Stage 1, 97, 126
Key Stage 2, 126

'Letterland', 5
Letters and Sounds guidance, 5, 6, 10, 71
lip-reading, 109
listening
  and remembering sounds, 16
  skills, 15, 16
littlelearners.education website, 118

Little Learners Education YouTube channel, 31, 44, 83, 85, 88, 112, 114, 117–118
'Little Wandle Letters and Sounds Revised', 10
long vowel sound, 127
loose parts, 127

'magic e', 61, 127
middle and end sounds, 48–49
misconceptions, 76
monosyllabic, 127

national curriculum, 127
National Literacy Strategy, 5
newly qualified teacher (NQT) survey, 3
nonsense words, 7, 81, 86

open compound words, 57, 122
open-ended activity, 127
oral segmenting and blending, 26–27

parent/carer involvement
　barriers to, 112–114
　common misconceptions about phonics, 112
　encouraging/supporting, 114–115
　importance of, 111
　phonics workshop for, 114, 115–116
past tense, 71–72
pedagogy, 128
Phase One phonics, 7, 15–28
　activities to support learning. See activities
　alliteration (aspect 5), 23–24
　assessment, 28
　body percussion (aspect 3), 20–22
　environmental sounds (aspect 1), 16–18
　instrumental sounds (aspect 2), 18–20
　oral segmenting and blending (aspect 7), 26–27
　revisiting, 27–28
　rhythm and rhyme (aspect 4), 22–23
　seven aspects of, 16–27, 121
　signs of gaps in, 28
　voice sounds (aspect 6), 24–26
Phase Two phonics, 7, 29–42
　accents, 39
　activities to support learning. See activities
　assessment, 41–42
　graphemes and phonemes, 30–33
　phonics session teaching, 33–37
　segmenting and blending CVC words, 37–38
　tricky words, 39–41
Phase Three phonics, 7
　accents, 50–51
　activities to support learning. See activities
　assessment, 53
　CVC words with digraphs, 48
　digraphs and trigraphs, 44, 46

　introduction to, 43–44
　middle and end sounds, 48–49
　phoneme frames, 47–48, 128
　sound buttons, 47
　sounds, 44–46
　tricky words, 51–52
Phase Four phonics, 7
　activities (for CCVC and CVCC words), 55–56
　assessment, 57–58
　CCVC and CVCC words, 54–56
　introduction to, 54–55
　polysyllabic words, 56–57
　writing, 57
Phase Five phonics, 7
　accents, 69
　activities for, 66–69
　alternative pronunciations, 66
　alternative spellings, 62–65
　assessment, 70
　introduction to, 59–60
　phonemes and graphemes, 60–62
　split digraphs, 61–62
　tricky words, 69–70
Phase Six phonics, 7
　activities for, 72–73
　assessment, 76
　comprehension, 75–76
　introduction to, 71
　misconceptions, 76
　spelling rules, 73–75
　suffixes, 72
　past tense, 71–72
phoneme frames, 47–48, 128
phonemes, 8, 29, 30–33, 60–62, 128
phonics, 1–11, 128
　common misconceptions about, 112
　continuous provision, 96–97
　further support and guidance on, 117–120
　learning
　　children with ADHD, 107
　　children with autism, 104–105
　　children with dyslexia, 105–106
　　children with hearing loss/deafness, 108–109
　　children with SEND, 103–109
　Letters and Sounds, 6, 10
　phases, 7. See also specific phases
　in provision, 95–102
　reasons for teaching, 5–6
　schwa, 8–9, 31, 112, 129
　segmenting and blending, 8, 26–27, 37–38, 130
　and SEND, 6, 82, 92, 103–109, 115
　session teaching, 33–37
　systematic synthetic phonics (SSP), 4–5, 10, 30–31, 101, 104, 109, 131

INDEX

validation, 9–10
workshop, 114, 115–116
PhonicsBloom.com, 120
Phonics: Everything You Need to Know, 119
phonics screening check, 128
   activity ideas to preparing for, 86–88
   criticism, 92
   exemption criteria, 89
   introduction, 81–82
   preparing for the check, 86
   structure, 82–86
   during the check, 89–91
   after the check, 91
PinkCatGames.com, 119
polysyllabic words, 56–57, 129
practitioner, 129
pre-prepared displays, 99
pronunciations, alternative, 66
provision, 95, 129
pseudo-words, 81, 87, 92, 128

quadgraphs, 76, 129
qualified teacher status (QTS), 100

real words, 73, 79, 81, 86–87, 128
Reception, 129
rest breaks, 90, 106
rhythms and rhymes, 22–23
rote learning, 4–5, 40, 112

scaffolding, 129
scheme-specific training, 119
schwa, 8–9, 31, 112, 129
segmenting and blending, 8, 130
   CVC words, 37–38
   oral, 26–27
short vowel sound, 130
sight words. *See* tricky words
simple past tense, 71
sound and word banks, 99
sound buttons, 47, 90, 130
sound out, 7, 8, 26–27, 130
sounds
   activities for specific, 35–37
   environmental, 16–18
   instrumental, 18–20
   listening and remembering, 16
   middle and end, 48–49
   Phase Three, 44–46
   talking about, 16
   tuning into, 16
   voice, 24–26
special educational needs and disabilities (SEND), 6, 82, 92, 103–109, 115
spellings
   alternative, 62–65
   rules, 73–75
   writing and, 57
split digraphs, 61–62, 131
suffixes, 72
summative assessment, 53, 58, 102, 131
systematic synthetic phonics (SSP), 4–5, 10, 30–31, 101, 104, 109, 131

Teachers' Standards, 100–102
'Teach your monster to read' app, 120
tricky words, 7, 122, 130, 131
   Phase Two, 39–41
   Phase Three, 51–52
   Phase Five, 69–70
trigraphs, 7, 44, 46, 48, 131
Twinkl.co.uk, 119
Twinkl Digest, 39

validation, 9–10
VC (vowel–consonant) words, 131
visual phonics, 90
voice sounds, 24–26
vowel digraphs, 44, 132
vowels, 132

weekly information sheets, 114
Wendon, Lyn, 5
word banks, 99
working displays, 98–99
workshops, for parents and carers, 114, 115–116
writing, 57

YouGov, 3

www.ingramcontent.com/pod-product-compliance
Lightning Source LLC
Chambersburg PA
CBHW051410070526
44584CB00023B/3374